the
Queen
of Gay
Street

The Queen of Gay Street

by
Esther Mollica

Published by IDÉE FIXE BOOKS
Printed in the United States of America

Cover design & typesetting by semnitz™ at 99designs.com

To the editor who said I'd never sell a single copy of this book. I'm pretty sure I've now sold at least two copies.

My deepest and most heartfelt gratitude to: Kristen & Maria & Tita & Sara & Lauren & Stephanie & Eva & Sue & Jill & David & The Editorial Department & Whitney & Nanowrimo & Paragraph NY & Aaron & Rena & Jessica & Kat & Shannon & Greg & Kate & Grace & Gena & Juliet.

The dice of love are shouting and madness.
—Sappho

Contents

Chapter
1

An Empire State of Mind

There wasn't anything left for me in San Francisco. San Francisco didn't have enough romance and glamor. It became too familiar, like a lover who swapped her best date night outfits for mom pants and morning breath. I was thirsty for New York's brazen, sadistic wiles.

I was born and raised in the Tenderloin, the worst area of The Golden City—my first memories as a child were of walking past prostitutes and heroin addicts in the Tenderloin on the way to school.

Even though it was my hometown, I'd never felt a sense of belonging. I'd never known people to be more fake than the card-carrying PETA members who were as cruel to other human beings as they were caring to animals. Every day was a protest. Every day someone had to complain that the world remained imperfect. Every day I had to sidestep literal piles of human shit and vomit on the way to work and deal with homeless people calling me a fatty or a bourgeois asshole—or just telling me to go to hell. Once I bought a slice of pizza for a homeless man on Haight Street. He told me I was an inconsiderate bitch, that he was gluten intolerant and a vegan, then threw the slice on the ground. Another day, I passed by a guy shouting, "Get your anti-capitalism shirts here! Fifteen dollars!"

San Francisco became my personal *Groundhog Day*. I felt irritated whenever tourists asked me if the Bay Bridge was the Golden Gate Bridge, whenever outsiders pointed and laughed at the man in a giant pineapple suit playing the ukulele, and whenever panhandlers asked for money while unabashedly typing away on a brand-new MacBook Air.

New York wasn't anything like that. She called to me with her wayward charms. On so many visits, I was enchanted by the breathless grace of wandering the city in the dark. The way we fit together so perfectly, intellectually and culturally, spooning so that the city filled in the places where I was hollow. On one vacation I went to the Oscar Wilde Bookshop on Pride weekend, and a girl totally strung out on E outside of the store said, "I promise if you buy a book, I'll show you my tits!" I bought a book, and she shoved her bare breasts in my face while three girls cheered. Unadulterated literacy? Motorboating outside a bookstore that felt more like a bawdy saloon? Sign. Me. Up.

A year later, during The Great Recession of '08, I got laid off from my cushy digital-marketing job for PlayStation. In its place I began working a job processing paperwork for the government, getting paid close to nothing.

Despite the terrible pay, big shifts were afoot in my department, and I finally had a boss who really liked me and who I got along with. After only a handful of months she said she wanted to promote me to an accounting position and double my annual pay to $60,000 (which, for an English major during the recession, was a king's ransom.)

Yet it wasn't a raise that guided my next decision.

I'd fallen hard for a girl from the Windy City who *blew me away*. Morgan and I met in an online writing community, where we always chatted about how we'd meet up "someday" in San Francisco. In 2005 we'd wooed, hooked up, and continued a long-distance off-and-on dalliance. But even when we were "off," I never really wanted anybody but her. Finally, I put everything on the line. I thought, *This time, there won't be any other lovers. Let it be just you and me or nothing at all. Let's end this game.* I garnered my courage to tell her how I felt and flew to Chicago.

It was there that I had my heart broken. And soon after I learned the real reason why. The greatest love of my life was married—to a man—and had lied to me about being gay for three years.

After that, quitting my job didn't seem like a hard decision, even though I'd be turning down money when I needed it most. I sold every single thing I had that was nonessential and fit the rest into two backpacks. Somehow, moving three thousand miles away to a place where I knew not one soul seemed like the best solution to my feeling of being adrift. Probably because I wasn't afraid of being alon—I felt alone every night when I came back from the Lex to an empty apartment.

So I took a three-day trip to New York to set myself up for a new life. On day one, I rented the first apartment I laid eyes on in Astoria and secured all my basic furniture needs from Ikea. The next day, I built my furniture in a Hooters wifebeater while blasting Kat DeLuna's, "Run the Show" with the base turned up to eleven. And I fantasized. I fantasized about meeting a New

York femme at a goddamned book club. They existed here. After all, wasn't New York's motto basically, "Give me your tired, your poor, your undersexed"?

At that point in my life, I didn't think I could fail. Love would be here in the biggest city in the United States—how could it not be? A new job in publishing and journalism would be waiting just for me—no doubt about it.

So I quit my job. Then I slipped a letter under my landlord's door. I said my goodbyes, put the cat in a carrier, and hopped on a one-way flight to my new home in Astoria. My furniture was already set up from that three-day weekend, and two bags were not that hard to unpack.

By the time I was fully settled into my new place, it was about ten o'clock at night. I grinned and realized that I could still go to a club. In San Francisco the party would be dying in about two to three hours. But in New York City, it was just beginning.

Looking out the window, I saw that it was beginning to snow. I had no appropriate shoes and didn't know anything about this mysterious white substance falling from the sky. It never snowed in California. So I interpreted this as a delightful miracle, hailing my arrival. With nowhere else to buy winter footwear, I went to a discount outlet shop in my neighborhood, got a pair of black boots with tacky fur on them, and rode the train into Manhattan, where the snow was about halfway up my leg when I got out of the station.

Trudging through the ice, I made it all the way to my first lez bar. It was now eleven o'clock. The night was still young. And this would be my very first night out as a real New Yorker.

A girl shoved her way past me as I waited in line for the bouncer to check my ID. She was shouting, "I *hate* this city! I hate everything about it!"

I wasn't jaded or afraid of strangers yet (like any real New Yorker), so I said, "Hey, do you wanna talk about it?"

"This city is shit!" she screamed. "I moved here a year ago. The whole place smells like urine and garbage; it's dirty. There are rats everywhere. *And don't get me started on the women!*"

"The women?" I said. "But that's the whole reason I moved here! Today's my first day."

She stared at me like I was a crazy person.

"Enjoy it. I'm going home. I have wasted my entire life here."

She threw her cigarette onto the ground while the bouncer and a couple of butches smoking outside cackled.

"Go home, honey. Don't let the door hit you on the way out!" they shouted.

I stepped inside, where the DJ was blasting "Empire State of Mind." I felt it. There was nothing I couldn't do in this concrete jungle.

It was a far cry from the depressing Ani DiFranco songs on the jukebox at the Lex. This was a whole bar full of power lesbians in black dresses and suits. Everyone smelled like success and department-store perfume. Not patchouli! I looked around and saw the other girls wearing actual heels, staring disdainfully at my feet (which now looked like two soggy, dead Muppets.)

This is great, I thought. *Now I'm definitely not the only asshole at the bar. I'm home, ladies. I'm home.*

Chapter
2

Age Before Beauty

When my taxi first rolled in from the airport, I dragged my two duffel bags out of the trunk and stared at my new apartment building. Stark, dingy, almost Soviet. It was cheap and sad like many of the apartments in New York, but it was also right around the corner from a subway stop to Manhattan, and it was just a quick jaunt to Steinway Street. In San Francisco, I'd had the good fortune of living in a crappy area of the Mission that accidentally became a hipster mecca—evidenced by the budget fast-food restaurant across from my apartment suddenly being turned into a bougie dining hall that served fifteen-dollar scoops of Humphry Slocombe ice cream. That had been another sign that it was time to leave. I wondered if the same thing would happen to Astoria, Queens.

I stepped inside, juggling my luggage and heard a voice call from down the hall. Signs of life from my first neighbors in New York.

"Would you like to buy a vibrator? You look like you could use one!"

A middle-aged woman wearing tight latex pants appeared in her apartment's doorway. She was swirling a glass of white wine and had a smile plastered on her face.

"Ever been to a toy party? It's not as weird as you think. It's like a Tupperware party for *just us girls.*"

The frosted blonde appeared to be north of forty-five. Was she a girl? Was I? My new apartment was on a street full of mostly Greek retirees and discount-clothing shops that were hanging by a thread. Why was a solicitor trying to sell me dildos? This wasn't the Gayborhood.

An old woman in front of the unit to her left scowled as she flicked a broom across her doormat with a mix of righteous disapproval and anxiety.

"That's my daughter," the middle-aged woman said as a younger version of herself struggled toward us with two armfuls of clear plastic bins, not even attempting to hide their contents.

"Mom! You're embarrassing me! Don't invite strangers to the party!"

"It's fine, honey. This is about women helping each other out! Supporting a woman-owned business! Living your sex life on your own terms! Here, take my business card."

She handed me a gold-embossed card that featured a suggestively shaped pear. I thought about her initial greeting. *"You look like you could use one."* Apparently my lack of a love life was starting to show. I thought of the *Sex and the City* episode about Charlotte's depressed vagina. Still, I wouldn't buy dildos from a stranger. It was weird.

"Sex is for marriage!" the old woman suddenly squawked. "What kind of values are you parading in front of your daughter?"

"Nobody cares. Fuck off," the girl said, shoving the last of the boxes into her apartment and slamming the door.

"And did you know your daughter is an *alcoholic?!*" the old woman shrieked, banging the edge of her broom against her neighbors' apartment door.

None of this was strange to me. My neighbor in San Francisco was a shy, gay coder who ended up slowly morphing into a leather daddy after his partner died. He used to come over and ask me which of his assless chaps showed off the goods best. This was tame in comparison.

The old woman set her broom against the wall.

"So, are you the new tenant the super mentioned? Are you moving into the apartment on the third floor?"

"Yes," I said. "I'm from California, actually. This is my first day in New York."

"I'm a lifelong New Yorker," the old woman said, beaming with pride. "My name's Trudy. I'll be here if you need anything. I hope you like it here! And also," she added, lowering her voice to a whisper, "when anything goes on in this building, I'm the first to know about it."

As I pulled my duffle bags up to the third floor, I thought, *What's not to like?* I'd just been accosted by a shady saleswoman trying to peddle fake dicks for an extra buck. And I'd met an old woman apparently skilled in low-key espionage.

It didn't take long to unpack. Eventually, I put the last of my clothes into my drawer and decided to go back down to talk to Trudy before going out and having a drink. I knocked on her door. On the other side, I heard the great yowl of a cat as Trudy came to the door and answered.

"Oh! I didn't expect to see you again so soon," she said. "Don't you want to go out and explore the city?"

"I thought about it," I said.

"Well, I hope you aren't going to go out wearing that. You should take better care of yourself, dear." She raised the tip of her cane at me. "A man won't want you, not looking like that."

I didn't know how to tell Trudy that I didn't give a shit what men thought. However, I didn't want to look terrible in front of women. I was wearing discounted jeans from Ross Dress for Less and a graphic tee bearing the logo of a fictional saloon.

"There's still time to get some new clothes before you go out," Trudy said, as she suddenly shot up and began to chase a chubby brown cat in circles around the apartment. "I just don't want you to be embarrassed, that's all. Appearances matter, you know!"

I hadn't been in the city long, and the first two New Yorkers I'd had conversations with very bluntly let me know that (a) I looked as if I hadn't had sex in a long time (I hadn't) and (b) I resembled a hobo incapable of finding love. It was refreshing.

She invited me in. I sat down on her couch, which was a dull pink color and covered in floral doilies.

"I can't catch Tabitha," Trudy said, sighing. "Would you like a cup of tea?"

"Yes, please."

Trudy went into the kitchen. After she left, Tabitha jumped onto my lap. The cat gave me a panicked look and purred loudly. Her eyes said, "Please save me."

Trudy shuffled back into the room with two cups of tea.

"Aha!" she cried. In one motion, suspiciously fast for her age, she picked up a satin bow from a side table and placed it around the cat's neck. Tabitha now looked like a Christmas present. The cat wailed again as though she were in pain and ran under the couch.

"Tabitha likes you, I think," Trudy said. "She hardly ever comes out; she's shy." I didn't have the heart to tell Trudy that the cat probably just didn't like her, specifically.

"She keeps me company now that my husband's gone. He was a good man; we just passed our fifty-year anniversary. I found him dead of a heart attack one morning."

"I'm sorry," I said. "I can't imagine how badly it hurts to lose someone after that long."

"I've made my peace with God," Trudy said. "We had a good life together. We raised one daughter. Not everyone can say that, you know. That they met someone who loved them in this life. It just feels as if I don't know what to do with myself anymore. What I should do with my days. But that's enough about me. Tell me why you came to New York."

I told Trudy about my dreams to become a writer in a place so glittering and grand. Omitting gendered pronouns, I told her I'd fallen in love with someone who lied about being married and decided to reinvent myself, fix my life.

"Men never change," she spat. I wanted to correct her and tell her that I was gay, but I knew that hers was another generation, another time. And I didn't want to land her in a matching grave with her husband.

"I'd better get going," I said. "This was nice. I hope we can visit again. Thank you for the tea."

Trudy gave me a hug.

"If you go around the corner, up Steinway Street, you can still find a place to buy new shoes. Goodbye, dear."

From this interaction, Trudy, an elderly woman in her eighties, became the first friend I made in New York. After a month I went to a locksmith and gave Trudy an extra key. The next day, I came home from job hunting to find the entire apartment enrobed in gaudy peach curtains and floral-printed quilts.

"I had a few things in storage; I thought you might need

something to decorate your apartment! I hope you like it," she said. Later, I took the blankets and curtains and hid them in the closet, thinking it would be impossible to get laid in a bachelorette pad that looked like the set of *Mama's Family*. Whenever she said she was coming over, I'd quickly put everything out again so as not to hurt her feelings.

When I was still new and feeling somewhat alone, watching AMC at Trudy's on Friday evenings became a habit. I always had fun with her, but inevitably she'd say something racist and I'd make a polite exit.

"It used to be the Irish who ran the police force in this town. No one would dare run afoul of an Irishman on patrol. And the races didn't mix as much back then."

"I'm not feeling well. Goodbye, Trudy."

Previously I barely knew how to cook a packet of noodles or boil eggs, but I somehow became obsessed with the idea of making a peanut butter cheesecake and bringing it to Trudy's for one of our classic TV marathons at the end of the week. On the nights when I was more scared of dancing with strangers than dying alone, I hurled all my efforts into researching recipes until, finally, I made the perfect dessert.

"You can't give me this!" Trudy shouted when I brought the cheesecake over. It wasn't the reaction I'd expected.

"Are you diabetic?"

"No!" she thundered. "I thought we were trying to find you a man! Do you think you'll get married with an ever-expanding waistline? Well, you won't."

"I'm not worried about getting married," I said.

"You're almost *too* old for marriage," she chided coolly.

Maybe it was because of my period, but I teared up a bit at her words.

"Oh dear, I'm so sorry, I'm just concerned for you," Trudy said as she gave me a hug. "I want you to know that God sees you. You aren't alone in this world. And I see you too."

I didn't know how to tell her that she didn't see me—not really. Because if she did, she'd accept that I was gay and biracial. And if she didn't see me, maybe God didn't either. I also wanted to tell her that it wasn't faith in God that would save this world; it would be people's faith in one another. Like faith in the unspoken bond that I'd come visit her on Fridays so she wouldn't have to talk the ear off the mailman, the super, or any other human being who came to her door—and neither of us would have to face the terror of the loneliness that threatened to swallow us whole.

"I'm not feeling well. Goodbye, Trudy."

Chapter
3

Below Zero

I still remember the first blizzards. How cold it was during my first winter in New York. How, just before the cold hit, someone at a bar ominously said, "Beware the culling."

"What's the culling?" I asked.

She responded, "It's when every single lesbian in New York pairs off because they don't want to be cold and alone at night. But don't worry; when summer hits everyone gets dumped because people then regret their choices."

One by one, the culling claimed lesbians from the usually busy bar. Soon the only people who remained were me and two fifty-year-olds getting wasted on an empty dance floor. Some nights were so cold and dark that I longed a little for death. I couldn't even hook up with anyone; even though we hadn't spoken to each other for almost a year, I was still in love with Morgan and feeling confused. When I finally did hook up with somebody, I didn't feel alive. The sex made no difference at all.

When I met Morgan, I was instantly beguiled. It's creepy to say that because we had the same haircut, would wear the same outfits, and had the same birthday (we were born five minutes apart). When she visited me in San Francisco, multiple people asked us if we were twins. Eventually, she got tired of it and told somebody, "Yes, we are, and we make billions in the porn industry."

We had the same taste in music, the same humor, the same taste in art. This was a girl who went to the symphony and opera by herself. This was a girl who, with her long dark hair and gothy bangs, her fiery-red lips and sultry Italian good looks, laid me low at first sight. Like a young hart wounded in the thigh by cupid's arrow, I struggled to limp away from her innocent-yet-lusty charm. And she ensnared me without even trying.

We spent the whole weekend touring San Francisco, chatting excitedly about our favorite paintings at the art museums we visited. She wanted to hike to the top of Telegraph Hill to sketch parrots for her own paintings, and when we got there, I said, "Hey, look, there's Alcatraz" as if pointing out a prison would be really romantic. Shyly, she asked if I might like to come back to her hotel.

In her room we eyed each other, heavy with wine. And yet neither of us made a move. Like any typical Aries woman, we both made bawdy suggestions and talked a big game but were too afraid to follow through out of fear of rejection. So we watched "Yo Momma" on MTV for four whole hours, gripped by sheer terror. I think we both thought that if we just kept enduring the terrible jokes, neither of us would get our hearts broken. Eventually, after two hours, I got up the nerve to hold her hand. After three hours, I put my arm around her. After four hours, I gently slipped off her glasses and gave her a delicate smooch. We finally turned off the TV.

Maybe it was the creepy fact that we were each other's doppelgangers, but we seemed to have an innate understanding sexually. Again, with both of us being women of Mars, there was a meaty physicality to the way we caressed and pawed at each other. Yet there was no shortage of breathless declarations and sighs and holding each other through our releases. No Aries is a garden-variety slut; we're foolhardy harlots who want to be objectified for our bodies (because that's where our energy and power dwells) but not *just* for them. Any Aries girl will speak of the moon and the stars and all of heaven's hosts and swear upon anything it takes to seduce you. We'll make you feel like the only lover we've ever had in a procession of courtly love, for an Aries can't be moved except by something glittering and grand.

Sometimes, I feel you can touch and kiss a woman and sense one of the four elements in her energy. Morgan's was fire; every single touch on her delicate skin was so hot it hurt my heart to continue. I was consumed by her passions. I wanted every moment with her to last forever, for us to never stop sharing saltwater taffy at the wharves or avoiding mangled jellyfish on the shore at Ocean Beach. Her beauty was on another level, and it threatened to strike me dead every time I glanced at her. She was sweet in all the right places and brazen in the even better ones. Morgan fulfilled every part of me: emotionally, mentally, sexually. I never wanted that visit to end. I wanted to stay in her arms for always. When I curled up next to her, I felt both safe and challenged.

Everything about San Francisco made her eyes twinkle or grow big with awe. Whenever she opened her heart this way, mine opened with her. I had a sinking feeling that it couldn't be so easy, that in some obvious, Catholic way, I couldn't get this girl I wanted without suffering for her. Everything about her was bold and lively. Brazen yet innocent. When our flames touched, they only burned brighter, and the embers of my heart grew wild in a way that I knew would never cool.

She could quote courtly poetry but then say things like, "Get a Brazilian and stop shaving. It's like switching internet service providers; you will never regret it." Another time she said, "Let's go to New York together, just you and me. And let's get waxed; it will be hilarious. Getting double waxes in New York would be the ultimate femme bonding experience!"

Everything changed the day I flew out to Chicago.

Morgan was an eternal contradiction. A vegan obsessed with collecting taxidermy and animal skeletons for her paintings. Before making the trip, I bought a glass eye from a taxidermy store, put it in a ring box like I was going to propose, and hid it in my pocket. When she picked me up from the airport, I hadn't dressed properly for the cold and had nothing to cover my hands. She took off her own gloves, put them on me, and said, "You're such a typical California girl."

I blushed and said, "You're so chivalrous. I'll treasure your Smittens forever!"

We spent the whole weekend in art museums and arcades. I kept waiting for the right moment to give her my gift. Then, when we were standing out under the stars, waiting for a train to go back to my hotel, I whipped out the box without warning.

"I want you to have this," I said. "Because I love you and only have eyes for you."

Hesitantly, she took the box, then opened it. The glass eye just rolled around and around. She burst out laughing until she was out of breath and said, "Oh my God, this is amazing. I'm going to keep this in my house forever!"

Suddenly she looked frightened and stuffed the box into her pocket.

"I ah . . . I'm not feeling well. Look, I have to go. Um, I don't think we should see each other anymore. And I don't think we can be friends."

I couldn't fathom that three years of flirting was going to end this way, over what seemed to be a misunderstanding about a glass eye.

"Wait—Morgan. Can we talk about this?"

A train pulled up on the opposite side of the platform. She ran away from me, got on the train, and the doors slammed shut. I sat on the platform in disbelief as snowflakes began to fall into my hair.

Morgan didn't answer any of my texts or calls over the remaining two days of my visit to Chicago. I spent the rest of the weekend reading bad poetry at a feminist bookstore and sleeping. Eventually, I had to leave. On my way to the airport, I stopped at a kiosk that sold nothing but sandwiches and decided to ask for a BLT with triple the amount of bacon on it. *For every animal she saves, I'm going to eat three.*

I struggled to talk. "Excuse me. Can I have . . . a . . . sandwich with extra bacon on it? Like three fistfuls of bacon?"

Then I started crying. In public.

The cook rushed out, hugged me, and said, "Lady, you don't have to cry. It's just a sandwich!"

The whole flight home, I kept replaying the breakup in my head. At what moment had I gone wrong? I felt that there was more to the story. The sequence of events didn't make sense. So I started a rigorous Google search for answers, which led me to a Flickr account of hers that she'd never shared with me. It contained pictures of Morgan's wedding, which had taken place just a few months before I flew out to Chicago. She was married to a man and never told me. An artist from the same college where she had gotten her degree. And she went down the aisle in a green wedding dress and cowboy boots. I felt equal parts overwhelming rage, betrayal, and awe that another femme could pull off such a ridiculous outfit.

I wrote her a furious email, calling her out on her deception. She didn't respond with any explanation; all she could say was that she was sorry she'd lied for three whole years. It was too late to take any of it back. Our love was destroyed, our femme BFF friendship had vanished, and in its place was the horrifying realization that the person I'd spoken to on the phone every week for three years wasn't who I'd thought she was. She had made me feel like I wasn't alone in this world. She had been a person who'd also come out young and overcome the trials of being out on her own. Now she was just an illusion.

When I moved to New York, I felt like I had nothing left to lose. And I believed that challenging New York on my own was the only way I could learn to love something again with such passion, even if that thing was a city. Because loving someone so deeply and intensely, in such a way that seemed fated and now seemed false, had corrupted the deepest parts of my soul. I knew I would never love a girl the way I'd loved her. I stopped knowing the pleasures and sparks of attraction. Instead, I felt only fear—or worse: nothing at all.

Though I'd known my first drink, gotten my first piercing and tattoo, and experienced my first everything in San Francisco, all it took was the memory of being in Morgan's arms for my hometown to turn into an abandoned graveyard of old loves dangling from the hangman's branches while Telegraph Hill parrots flitted about through decaying trees. I knew I had to get up and feel something once more. And I convinced myself that if I moved to New York on my own and used all my energy just to survive, this love might stop wrecking me.

When I moved, I kept the Smittens.

One night during that first New York winter, I couldn't take being alone anymore. So I went to Death & Company by myself, batted away the affections of older men, and got drunk on a cocktail of vodka, egg whites, pineapple, and palm leaves. I loved it so much I ordered five. The world swayed and glistened; each star was burning just for me that night.

As I hailed a cab home, snowflakes started falling into my hair again. They made me think of Morgan. I wondered how her new life inside a closeted marriage was going. If "Esther, the insane lesbian" was just some gay whack job she once knew, not the girl she'd whispered to and kissed so passionately on business trips and mini vacays where we traveled across the country together. We'd shared everything together. And it had been a lie. How could I ever trust another woman again?

I shook the snowflakes out of my hair as I stepped into the cab, then starred out the window while continuing to think about that night in Chicago at the train station. The cab driver spoke to me in the Queen's English. Many of the Global South countries that mandate English lessons teach an overly proper, antiquated form of the language. My Filipino grandmother once said, "Esther, mayhap a young man shall court you? You need only find one who does not gallivant to and fro."

"My lady," the cab driver said, looking into his rearview mirror. "What troubles you so upon this evening?" I thought about how he'd said it so earnestly. *"My lady."* Morgan had called me that when we took a trip to New York together, after she stepped forward to offer me her umbrella in the rain. No one had ever called me a lady before. And certainly no one ever made me feel like one.

"Nothing," I said, trying to not give away too much personal information to a stranger.

"No, my lady," the driver pressed, "I have not seen eyes so sad in so very long. Who is it that you love?"

"Ah! So you knew it all along, I see."

"Yes, my lady. No one has that look if it is not a look of lost love."

"Well, I loved someone who lied about being married for

three years, and I got screwed hard—I doubt there was enough 'love' to go around in that situation."

"No, my lady. If it was you who loved, and loved truly, then the love was real. Think not of the past. The city may bring you a new admirer any day now."

I made it through three blizzards my first year. I stayed and survived even though I had never known snow. And even after the barflies said, "Go home, Miss California. Ya ain't gonna make it out here!"

On another night I went for a long walk at three o'clock. I told myself I would rather freeze than go home to an empty apartment. So I wandered and wandered. All over the village, all over Queens. My ears felt like they were going to fall off. I told myself, *I won't go home; I will let this cold pierce me until I stop feeling anything at all.* It didn't work. Turns out, my emotions are stronger than a blizzard.

Finally, I realized I couldn't beat the elements anymore, and frost-bitten fingers would be the equivalent of a lady castration. That night was the hardest. I went home and cried. I didn't know how I would make it in New York on my own. I wondered if the move had been a mistake.

Still, the next day, I put one foot in front of the other and kept going. And I finally learned that, no, you can't beat a blizzard in one evening. But the ice has to melt eventually.

Morgan wrote a poem comparing me to springtime, and I'd kept it with me, along with the Smittens. It was the only poem I'd ever received from a girl.

I thought, *Hmm, springtime can thaw the snow. All I have to do is wait. All I have to do is stay alive.* Then I reached into my pockets and pulled out the Smittens. I touched part of them to my face one last time, walked to a dumpster close to the nearest subway, and threw them away.

Chapter
4

The World's Oldest Profession

In the full bloom of spring, I decided it was time to get out there—or at least take one step toward dating again. So I took two trains to the deepest recesses of Brooklyn to meet a girl I'd connected with online. She was quirky, with big glasses and an asymmetrical mullet. And she'd just moved to the city from Ohio.

When we got to the place she'd picked, I asked for one thing: a single cup of tea that cost one dollar. She whined and complained that she shouldn't have to pay a dollar; we should each be responsible for our own costs. I gently reminded her that I had taken public transportation for an hour and a half to meet her. She threw up her hands, paid the dollar, and then spent the next thirty minutes complaining about how she would no longer be able to make rent.

"Just so you know, I'll now be overdrawn exactly one dollar. If I end up on the street, it will be because of you," she said.

Due to my chronically low self-esteem in my twenties, I went home with her anyway. She lived in a converted open floor plan warehouse with four other hipster artists. They had divided their rooms by hanging towels on clotheslines or making clever use of cardboard. Even her restroom didn't have a door; a bedsheet marked that the toilet was in use.

She made me dinner (a slightly raw hamburger patty slapped on a plain bowl of boiled spaghetti noodles with no sauce) and wondered why I wasn't eating. I didn't want to tell her that I greatly feared food poisoning and shitting my brains out in a bathroom that was essentially a hipster's outhouse gone horribly wrong.

Then we went out on the rooftop of the warehouse and looked at the city while she talked about how she couldn't believe she'd finally made it here. "Out under the stars with a beautiful girl . . . I couldn't ask for more, even if I really won't be able to make that rent check on Monday."

She later played the guitar beautifully and wanted to hook up that night, but I wished her well and rode the train an hour and a half back to Astoria. I wondered if I was being high-maintenance, if demanding someone pay one dollar for me to enjoy a sack of leaves in boiled water made me a horrible princess.

I always figured straight girls had it easier. They had more selection, more privilege. They never ran out of an endless supply of men to date, and I felt men were very uncomplicated because I, too, believed video games, boobs, and random penetration would lead to a happy and fulfilling life. Conversely, I told friends about dates with girls who had shown up on heroin, dates where women had disclosed that they had husbands or were still living with their girlfriends, dates where girls I barely knew tried to get me into threesomes. Every date had some element of bizarre or crazy, no matter if I met the girl at a volunteering event or on the untamed wilds of the internet.

Meanwhile, my straight friends would say, "Yeah, I went on a date with this boring guy. And I hated his *ugly shoes*."

Hettie girls, I deduced, also never had to pay for anything. In all of their stories the men held open doors, wined and dined them, and absorbed the entire check—even if the men proceeded to never call. I figured dating a man was exactly like being a Safeway Club Card rewards member. My God, think of the savings over ten years of dating! Men also at least had to pretend they were interested in more than just sex out of fear of looking like a douchebag. Lesbians basically just flashed me a V tongue gesture after the first cocktail. And, more often than not, I went along with it because I felt the old adage of "Why buy the cow when you can get the milk for free?" only applied to men.

I know the process of trying to find a mate is full of false starts—or worse—for all people. I also know that trying to discover your common interests and determine if the other person knows where your G-spot is on the first date isn't a successful strategy. I know because I did it to death.

If I were better about being casual, I might have sidelined a lot of impending heartache. But I was both extremely picky and extremely cavalier about who I went home with and why. Dating was an eternal chicken-and-egg struggle between my insatiable horniness and my desire to place my chin in my hands, prop my elbows on a table, and endlessly dote on the right girl's capacity for wit and grace. What I was looking for in a hookup was someone who would beat me into submission with her talent or intelligence and exist at the level of a goddess, at which point, the idea of being casual was basically nixed. How could I be casual with someone formidable? I could never just meet someone I had an ambivalent attraction to and ask them to spread for me. That was too clinical, about as sexy as someone saying, "Put 'em in the stirrups; you can keep your socks on."

I had a system for enforcing my standards. If someone was super hot and witty, to hell with the fact that she was chronically depressed over her ex-girlfriend. Time to fuck! If someone was excellent at talking dirty and had her MFA, who cared whether or not she was on meth? *Sit. On. My. Face.* But if someone was boring yet wanted a relationship? Or maybe just a little plain but looking for a girlfriend? I wouldn't sleep with *that* person.

Then, after I did sleep with someone, large amounts of oxytocin would surge through my brain, and I would be convinced that the addict, the player, the married woman, the girl who wanted nothing but a one-night stand was *the one*. In this way, I selected only the best of the worst.

So I kept putting myself out there, all night long, going to these bars and waiting for that magic spark and perhaps some earth-shattering sex with someone who didn't really feel like a stranger. It almost never happened. Generally, the night ended at around three or four o'clock with me drunk, missing someone who had broken my heart several years before for no real reason, and not getting laid. And then a disgusting man asking me to go home with him as I made my way to the nearest subway or taxi. Usually, the less-promising the night had been, the grosser the guy was.

Once, on a long trip back to Queens after a long night of clubbing, a strange man approached me on the train. He'd stared at me for a long time across the aisle and then suddenly pulled out his phone, walked over, and placed it in my hand.

The phone screen said: "Hello. I am deaf. Can I get your number? I can't stop looking your way, and I love that ass in those jeans, *mamí*. That. Ass."

I didn't know how to turn him down. Other than being horribly crass, I found his courage incredibly endearing.

"Thank you," I typed back. "Married. Four kids."

He left me alone after that, and I enjoyed the rest of the ride back in peace. Yet that night still wasn't over. As I walked back to my apartment, I began to hear heavy breathing behind me. Then the jangling of chains.

A morbidly obese man was wheezing as he struggled along on his bicycle. Even as he pumped his legs as hard as he could, he barely kept up with my stride. "I . . . damn," he huffed. "I thank . . . God . . . that he . . . made women . . . like you. What . . . I got . . . to do . . . to get that ass? If you were . . . my girl . . . ain't no night you'd ever . . . not have my hands on ya."

I started to run as he pushed harder.

"Did I . . . scare you? Come back!" he cried.

I ran as fast as I could until he disappeared into the distance, then slammed the apartment door behind me.

That night, I somehow concluded that the women who charged had it made. It was clear to me at twenty-nine that no one would ever want me for anything other than my body. But I couldn't seem to capitalize on this or harness a relationship out of it. *I'm bad at marketing, I thought. A low-rent escort who is setting her prices too low. I need to expand my client list, garner high-yield and low-risk assets. Next time, I shall demand a large tea that costs two whole dollars!*

Even my mother cost more than I did. She was purchased from the Philippines in a mail-order marriage to a man who was clinically insane. Her mother, my grandmother, was bartered off in an arranged marriage to a stranger when she was fourteen years old. I wondered, *What the hell am I doing so wrong that I come from two generations of women whom men had to pay to marry, yet I'm not worth anything to women? My bedroom is operating in some sort of theoretical freemium model that appears successful but is secretly a failure. Like Spotify.* If you really think about it, love is just a transaction. And I wasn't making enough from it anymore.

Chapter
5

Mommy Dearest

My mom was the first high-maintenance femme I ever encountered who didn't love me. She isn't a horrible person. She just has a cluster B personality disorder—specifically, borderline personality disorder. My father, on the other hand, was a diagnosed narcissist and sociopath. Two totally different people drawn together from two totally different cultures, they had no real capacity for empathy, yet their reasons for not having the key component to normal relationships with other people differed.

My dad was always cold, selfish, and bragging about how he was the smartest person in the room, while my mom was always laughing the loudest, telling stories with the greatest theatrics, and showing off. At school, people teased me and said she looked like Ms. Swan on Mad TV. She constantly wore athletic wear paired with gaudy jewelry, despite not ever wanting to set foot in a gym. At times she seemed like the Asian Jessica Simpson and not the brightest bulb in the box. But she took me aside one day and said, "Esther, sometimes you just have to let men think you are stupid. That's how you keep them."

Both during and after marriage, my mom and dad constantly fought and screamed at each other. Two Scorpios do not make a right. I find it ironic that they both were born under the symbol of death and I was born under the symbol of birth. They were loud and hit below the belt with their insults. The only time their arguing ever got physical was one night when my dad slapped my mom in the face. She quickly grabbed my umbrella, which had a wooden head shaped like a baby hippopotamus, and beat him with it, creating such a large head wound that he had to go to the hospital and be treated for a concussion.

At that point it was pretty apparent I already hated my father. All I said was, "Mom, you broke my umbrella."

The two of them made everything into a power struggle. Frequently, they argued about who *wouldn't* have to take care of me. Once I started vomiting at school in fourth grade, and the office begged both my parents to come pick me up. Nobody came because they were arguing over who *wouldn't* have to do it.

Another time, I had strep throat and needed to go to the doctor. In the days of landlines, it was possible for me to pick up a phone and hear my mom talking on the other line.

"Well I shouldn't be the one to take her," she said.

My father responded, "If you drop her off at my house, I will leave her at an orphanage. See if you want it that way."

I resented my mother for constantly acting weak to entice men. When my father touched me inappropriately for the first time, I was five or six. He and I were watching TV, and I felt his hand travel between my legs. I screamed and ran into the living room, where I told Mom what had happened. All she did was come into the room, frown, and say, "Please don't do that again." And that was it. My mother had the will of an ancient Waray warrior. The Waray, the tribe my family descended from, are known well throughout the Philippines for being the most hotheaded and hot-blooded. If my mom wanted to yell at customer service for not letting her return a sweater on day thirty-one within a thirty-day return policy, there would be hell to pay. But if my dad touched my pussy, it was just, "Please don't do that again," as though he'd left the toilet seat up.

I don't doubt that my mom cared for me. It was just not in a healthy, normal way that a mother should love her child. She didn't show up even once to any of my sports games. In high school, I'd run up and down the basketball court and search the stands for my family. No one was ever in the crowd. I was a terrible athlete, despite winning "Best Sportsmanship" every year, so it was incredibly rare when I got sent out onto the court, and it usually only happened because we were already losing and the coach felt sorry for me. I was always so excited to charge out and try my hardest—but there was never anyone to cheer me on. Ironically, the only person who sometimes came to my games was my father. Once when he sat in the stands, two boys waxed poetic about my ass, then said, "Number fourteen is so hot; but give her the ball and the game's over." He flew into a rage and screamed at the boys for talking about my body. I wondered why that mattered so much to him.

When I started to go through puberty, my mother was critical of my body and looks yet often bought shoes or clothes that were three to four sizes too large for me. Meanwhile, she'd buy the finest in shitty jewelry from at-home shopping networks for herself. She eventually had to declare bankruptcy from buying so many things on TV that she had an entire suitcase of full bracelets, which might as well have been fool's gold. Often, she opened the bag just to look lovingly at her cheap jewelry. Then she'd put it back in the closet again.

The materialism was what finally drove me away from her. Although my mom had primary custody, every weekend that I had to see my dad he would abuse me or expose me to sexual things (it's not really a fatherly thing to drive around town with your thirteen-year-old daughter while blasting "Lick It" and boasting about the hot Filipino prostitutes you fucked on vacation.) But if I didn't see my dad, my mom wouldn't get her child-support payments, which meant less money for her to spend on herself. I frequently went hungry because she bought food she wanted and not the healthy food I needed to grow. Dinner might be a greasy plate of bacon or a plate of pig's fat, and if I didn't like it, I was being an ungrateful, picky American who needed more variety in her diet. My breakfast every morning was exactly one piece of toast and hot cocoa. When I was sixteen, I weighed ninety pounds. Teachers were disturbed, and multiple people asked if I was anorexic. I wasn't anorexic. I was hungry and not being fed at home.

Still, I had a savior. My grandmother on my father's side was my own fairy godmother. She knew that my dad had mental problems and that a mail-order bride wasn't exactly real marriage material. So for nearly half of every year, I went to live with her in Kansas. I think this was my grandmother's way of trying to redeem herself; she'd had a terrible battle with alcoholism in her youth and wasn't around much to take care of my father. The way she told it, my dad just had so many problems (in retrospect, indicative of his sociopathy), which included harming other kids and animals. She had no choice but to send him to military school. But when my dad tried to pull his usual shit on boys who were bigger than him, he was sodomized. And this kept happening—multiple times for entire years—until he tried to run away from the military school. My grandmother never forgave herself for not being there for him, so she did her best to be a good mother for me.

Every year, I would alternate between living in low-income, urban environments and a charmed, suburban life in Kansas. My grandmother's house was large, and she had a Labrador retriever named Duke, who was my companion. In Kansas, I had friends my age, and we climbed trees together. "Oma" fed me three healthy, square meals a day. If not for her, I probably would have become just as messed up as my parents—she was the only person in the world who protected and guided me throughout my childhood.

My grandmother was a painter obsessed with art, and we would spend days drawing horses and squirrels together. Though I wasn't artistically inclined, I ended up developing a deep love for the art galleries we frequented. The Nelson-Atkins Museum of Art wasn't far from her place; not many people know that one of the largest, finest art museums in the country is located in Kansas. I think my love for Morgan was somehow psychologically tied to this part of my life—that her wholesome Midwestern charm and extensive knowledge of art recalled something deep in my soul from the one happy part of my childhood. Whenever Morgan imparted her knowledge on me, I never wanted her to stop talking, never wanted to stop exploring. Morgan was the only person in my tragic adulthood who made me feel like a kid again.

Nothing was dysfunctional about my trips to America's heartland except for my German step-grandfather. My biological grandfather died years before I was even born and was an alcoholic who viciously abused my grandmother until she was forced to leave. My step-grandfather wasn't violent, but he was an alcoholic too. He erred more on the loving side and would stay up all night drinking, slurring, and telling ridiculous stories. A few times he watched porn in front of me. But he never touched me, at least. He also would complain about Germany losing World War II and talk about his good old days in the Nazi Youth Leagues. He frequently argued that biracial people were not what God intended, and when I brought up that I was biracial, he said, "It's okay; you're a good color."

My mother sent me over there—every single year—without once getting on a plane with me. I was six years old the first time I had to ride on that plane by myself with only a teddy bear. She never explained why she did this, and even though she never offered to accompany me, she sure was the one to cry the hardest at the terminal each year.

As part of the "track system" at the public school I went to, breaks were divided for months at a time throughout the calendar year. My first visit was the hardest. My parents got divorced right before the summer and both decided to move to Stockton, two hours away. I was given no explanations as to why. I cried almost every night for a month, wondering where my mom had gone. My grandmother made a calendar and gave me a red pen, and she circled the day that I would go home, three months from then. She said, "Honey, I can send you home if you'd like, but how about every single day, you mark down one X on this calendar? If you can make it to the end, you will be a very strong person. And I think you are a very strong little girl indeed."

I kept putting X's on the calendar, every single day. And as the months went on, I stopped crying. I figured that if I never went home because my mom didn't really love me, that might be okay. My grandmother took better care of me and seemed to love me without conditions. Eventually, I did have to go back; my school operated on the "track" system. Instead of having one large summer vacation and winter break, they split the school year into time off every few months. So I was constantly shuffling between San Francisco and Kansas.

Over time, I noticed something happening to me. On some days, I felt like I was not really in my body or like I was not really real. No matter how much I cried, no one seemed to care or understand that so much uncertainty (and exposure to porn) was not good for me as a child. As an adult, when I looked at pictures of my childhood, I noticed a little spark in my eyes during my very early years—but it gradually faded. By the time that I was eleven, my eyes looked dark, sad, and full of hatred. I wasn't an unhappy person, and I still felt joy—but it wasn't naturally within me like it was before.

One day when I was about ten, I was in my room packing for another trip, and my mom entered. She theatrically burst out crying about how she wished I wouldn't have to get on that plane.

I turned to her and said, "Mom, you don't have to cry; I know you don't mean it. And when you say you love me, I know you don't mean it either. When you send me over there, it's just like sending a box in the mail."

That made her cry even harder.

A few months after my parents divorced, my mom started seeing a guy who was more of an asshole than my father. My dad was the cruelest person I've ever known, but he had passion. If I inherited anything from my father, it's the ability to fixate and get passionate about something. The new guy demanded I call him Dad and brought zero energy to our interactions. I refused to call him Dad, so we settled on the weirdly incestuous sounding "Uncle."

The only positive thing about him was that he never watched porn in front of me, which, apparently, was a tall order for the male father figures in my life. He never drove me anywhere or took me out to eat. If we went out for dinner, he and my mother would wait patiently while I took out an envelope of allowance money given to me by my grandmother and paid for myself. There's a part of me that loves to be spoiled by a femme daddy— and another part that wants to run away and throw up when it happens. Maybe this is why.

My new "Uncle" had no sense of fatherly duty but wanted the title. No sense of romanticism for my mother but demanded adoration. No conversational skills. I used to attempt to say hello to him, but he'd just pretend I didn't exist. Then he told my mother I was ignoring *him* and needed to be disciplined. My mother took his side, as always, because the only person in the room who could be right about anything was not, under any circumstances, a woman.

Soon the at-home dynamic of Mom allowing Dad to abuse me for crappy wristwatches, "Uncle" chain smoking and pretending I wasn't a real person became even worse with the addition of my Filipino grandmother, who came to live with us when I was twelve and frequently slapped or hit me for being "disobedient and American." My infractions could be as tiny as wearing makeup (of course, I was called ugly at school if *I didn't* wear makeup). Unsurprisingly, I didn't ever want to come home, whether from Kansas or just from school. My mom slowly developed a hoarding disorder that I started to notice around twelve, but became full-blown by the time I was fourteen. The floors went black with dirt, and the house was stacked from top to bottom with worthless items such as cereal boxes, Tupperware organizers, and lotion bottles. The only rebellious thing I ever did as a teenager was wake up at one o'clock in the morning and try to sneak all of the trash she was shoving into my room into a dumpster outside. I was grounded for cleaning my room.

I didn't want to be my mother, so I tried to be the opposite of her. Instead of relying on others for help, I resolved to do everything myself. She sat around doing nothing—I frequently overworked myself to the point of exhaustion. In high school I joined the debate club, basketball, women's football, and student council, and I took on volunteer work. My hope was that I'd have so many activities and friends' houses to go to that I wouldn't have to be home much. Home was a place to sleep, and that was it. My only goal in life was to get through the hell I was living in, both at home and at school—where everyone gossiped that I was a lesbian (I had no idea that everyone was right)—until I could leave and go to college.

My mother constantly needed more, more, more. More jewelry. More material possessions. I lived like a monk, with no more than I could carry in a backpack because I secretly never wanted to live in one place for very long.

After I went off to college, now back in San Francisco, my parents both seemed to go completely insane. My father was in and out of mental hospitals; my mother soon followed suit by experiencing auditory and visual hallucinations. "Uncle" called me and shouted that it was all my fault; no one would have ever gone crazy if I'd just stayed where I belonged and never tried to go to school. If they still had me to focus on and abuse.

I tried to call my mom in college. But I was also coming out, and no one in my life seemed to care or offer support. Going to clubs and coming home alone—or, alternately, only catching the eye of girls addicted to drugs or drinking—wore me down at a young age. I never visited my parents because I didn't want to deal with the verbal abuse and hoarding, so I worked my ass off in the city just to stay alive and hold my independence. One summer, I spent most of my time sleeping. When I was awake, I was either at work or a party, hoping someone at the next bar could notice and love me.

I told my mom all about the girl who raped me. About the girls at the club who needed money for drugs and alcohol, who stood me up or used me for sex. My mom would say, "Well, that's too bad," and ask if I would hang out with my dad so she could get another alimony payment.

I said, "Mom, I don't understand why all you care about is money. Money, money, money. If I killed myself over everything, I think your only reaction would be to complain about paying for the funeral."

My mother actually gasped and said, "Esther, haven't you set aside any savings in case that happens? I mean, I don't have the money to pay for a funeral. And I don't think I should have to."

Chapter
6

Fell Far from the Tree

In every bad 1950s lesbian pulp, the girl turns out gay because she had a horrible father. And if he's not horrible, he's at least "absent."

I wish I could say I had a great dad. A guy who smoked a pipe and wore fashionably nerdy glasses and encouraged his daughter every step of the way. I wish I could say I had the best father in the world because that "horrible father" stereotype is grounded in the archaic assumption that something "causes" a person to be gay. Let me be clear: even if I had that charming, nerdy, Mike Brady from *The Brady Bunch* type of dad, I still would have turned out this way.

Loving women is so intensely and innately woven into who I am that it couldn't have been a learned or taught behavior. When I was four years old, I said I wanted to wed Mary Poppins and fly around the world on adventures with her. So basically, nothing's changed.

I wish I'd had that "good dad." Instead, I had his perverse and sociopathic sibling. My father bought my mother from a mail-order bride catalog when he was thirty-six and realized no woman in her right mind would ever marry him. When he met my mom, he was sixteen years older than the pictures he sent through the mail. Apparently, this didn't bother her or set off any flags. When I asked my father why he chose my mom out of a catalog that looked much like the yearbook of an all-girls Asian high school, he said, "She had perfect teeth. They always said back home in Texas to choose a horse based on its teeth, for good breeding."

That was the reason he chose my mom. Breeding purposes. Not even because her profile indicated that her three interests were, "Reading, cooking, and listening to jazz." Hilariously, she likes none of these things (except for reading). When my mom came to America from the Philippines in the early '90s, she said Dad's family members told her, "He sometimes has episodes. Let us know if that happens."

My dad, like any textbook sociopath, feared only one thing: the judgment of death. Any self-help book on sociopaths will tell you that the sociopath fears death because it's the one inevitability they cannot charm, bargain, or strong-arm. Death comes for us all, even if you're good and pure, whether you're a virgin or a whore. So he spent his entire life saving up for a cryogenic capsule. He never once tried to own a home or a car, preferring to rent or borrow everything he had so he could afford to get frozen. Most parents save a little for their children's college education, maybe even their weddings. My parents didn't save a dime for mine.

My father constantly flew into rages where he screamed at everyone, howling about how incompetent and stupid they were. That used to be the thing he always screamed at me for—being stupid or boring.

Once he bellowed, "You're not going to get any guy with tits like those! *Grow them faster!*"

I responded, "Dad, I'm twelve."

It was then that his attacks shifted toward my looks and underdeveloped body. His eyes would flash with rage when he criticized me for not having a voluptuous body before I even got my first period. Whenever I told my mom about his anger over my lack of breasts, she would laugh and say, "Ho ho, your father and his sick jokes."

I remained underweight and nutritionally deficient throughout high school. This was because he constantly attempted to evade child-support payments, and my mom spent the few payments that did come through on tacky jewelry being sold on QVC.

When I was six years old, my mom divorced my dad for associating with criminals while practicing criminal law. He was a con man; I still have a love/hate relationship with *Better Call Saul* because I love Jimmy McGill, but he's too much like a funny and cool version of my dad. Which means he maybe isn't like my dad at all. Before my parents divorced, the three of us lived together in an apartment in the Tenderloin—the worst area of San Francisco. I walked into my first porn shop, a place called Frenchie's, at age four because there was a pink poodle on the door, and I thought it was a pet shop. For years we all slept together in the same bed. My father slept nude and refused to wear pajamas; I had to sleep with him on one side and my mother on the other. I guess it was too much for my mom to be a barrier.

My father was as physically disgusting as he was mentally. He was about three hundred pounds, and when I grew to be an adult, we were the same height. Five feet two. It was easy for him to scream at me—until we met eye to eye. He never took care of himself and hardly bathed, smelling like cheese or urine, the latter of which resulted from him peeing in apple juice jars and storing the liquid. Frequent seizures ailed him, and he took Dilantin. That caused his mouth to bleed, so sometimes when he smiled, his front teeth were coated in blood.

A man has never made my heart stir or my blood simmer; I have never once felt even a sliver of physical attraction to one. I can like guys as friends, I can give them awkward hugs, but I have never felt safe in a man's arms—and I distrust them enough that it's difficult to let a man get close to me.

My father was also a sex addict. Whenever I had to see him on Sundays for visitation rights, wayward women with sad eyes came banging on the door, asking for money in ragged clothes. Even as a child, I knew instinctively that something was wrong with this. Once he picked me up to go to the movies, and the back seat was splattered with his semen. I said nothing.

I know that my father did something to me. I remember him touching me, and I remember him watching porn in front of me. I don't remember what else, if anything, happened. My mom constantly took me to the doctor to be "inspected" in every orifice when I was younger and said it was routine.

I wonder: is letting your daughter be led unsupervised and alone into danger routine? As an adult, I now know this isn't normal. Nothing was ever wrong, so perhaps he never did more than touch me. Years later, I lay on a bed waiting for a girl who said I had posed so delicately it looked almost planned. She asked how I knew to lay so provocatively. My heart stopped; I knew that it must have been taught to me, and I said nothing.

Once we went to a car show when I was fourteen, and he suddenly lost his temper at me for "walking too fast." He beat me viciously with slaps and kicks in front of a parking lot full of people. They just stared. Except for one guy, who tried to stop it.

But his girlfriend held him back, saying, "Don't get involved" as my dad continued to hit and kick me.

That moment changed my life forever. Now, when I see another person in trouble, I charge in immediately because I learned that too many people are complacent. That it only takes one person to step in and end cruelty.

His beating finally ended after he hurled a cup of tea in my face, and three men, who'd been at a nearby bodybuilding competition, stopped to help.

Suddenly, my father cowered. For the first time in my life, he actually cowered before alpha males stronger and more authoritative than him. They offered to take me to their house and call the police, but I was afraid. I didn't know who these three men were, and I didn't want to be alone with them. So they put me in the back seat of my dad's car and took down his license plate number.

As we drove home, Dad said, "I'd offer you something to drink, but it seems I'm all out of tea." He chuckled.

"I hate you, Dad." It was the first time I ever told him how I felt. I was fourteen years old.

"I'm sure you do," he said, grinning like he was pleased with himself.

"When I grow up, I won't see you anymore. I'll leave, and I won't come back. You won't even be invited to my wedding. I'll have someone else walk me down the aisle."

He slapped his hands on the steering wheel and laughed uproariously.

"Like anyone would ever marry you!" he howled. "You're too ugly for anyone to ever fall in love with. You have no tits, no ass. You think any man would ever want to sleep with you? Ridiculous."

My heart sank, and on this day, I started to really hate myself. His words echoed through the years, and I began to fear I'd die alone. I hated everything about my face, everything about my body. I hated that I looked like him. Every time I looked in the mirror, I saw him laughing at me, mocking me.

My dad never stopped torturing me, and his side of my family endlessly praised him for being a good father. He did public charity work and was always in the papers as the local attorney with a heart of gold, fighting the good fight for homeless people and undocumented immigrants. Later, I found out he was running a sex trafficking website specializing in Filipino prostitutes. His family didn't care when he was later exposed on the news after San Joaquin started cracking down on Johns. He was still the ideal dad, and I was the disrespectful daughter.

Years later, in college, I tried to join a legal-advocacy group for minorities, and a woman with a clipboard said, "Oh! You're the daughter of Jack Zinn! He's done so much good work; your father is a champion!"

"He's no champion," I blurted out to a complete stranger. "He bought my mother; he works in sex trafficking. He abused me for years."

"You're a liar!" she screamed. "Your father is a *hero!*"

I walked away not volunteering for that group. But they called me every week, asking for help.

Throughout my college years, he sent letters every day telling me to give up on being a writer. That I had no story to tell and my ability was "worthless." Over time, the letters got stranger as his physical health noticeably deteriorated. He described the CIA coming after him and ringing his doorbell at night. Once he drove to campus to see me, sobbing heavily about seeing people's limbs blown apart in "the war" (he never served), and someone had to call security—he tried to drag me into his car because he'd come up with a plan to make me the "president of the United States," which meant that we had go to a local graveyard and dig up dead bodies together. Campus safety rescued me, and I considered a restraining order.

After that, he wrote to say that he now recognized my ability to write. He asked ever so sweetly if I could please write an entire book about *his* life because it would surely be a bestseller and not as boring as a book about *my* life.

I stopped talking to him because writing was the last thing I kept for myself. My entire life, my body, and my brain suffered from his abuse. I gave away the last of my heart to any girl who would fuck me at the local bar. I had nothing left anymore but my words, the last part of me that remained sacred and virginal, and he would not touch them.

Over and over, he begged on paper and on voicemail for me to come back. To come to the hospital. To please not let him die alone. I never bothered blocking him because, sadistically, I wanted to hear that begging. I started boxing at the local gym, training for fights to let out my anger. Every time I ran down the streets of San Francisco, I just wanted to keep running and never stop. Run away from him. Maybe run to something better.

The day he died I was sparring in a boxing gym. Bobbing and weaving, just dancing in the ring with a girl, when my mom walked into the gym. She'd driven from two hours away just to call out, "Esther, your father is dead."

I heard it out of the corner of my ear; a sudden frenzy of joy lurched and twitched in my heart. I lunged right past a punch aimed at my eye and threw a right cross into the other girl's face so hard that she fell backward and staggered against the ropes. That last punch landed at the perfect time. The coach called a time-out while the girl iced her face, and my mom looked on in horror.

"You're so violent. It's like you aren't my daughter anymore," she said.

"No, I'm more myself now than I have ever been. Now I'm free," I said.

She just stared.

"You're not sad that your father's dead?" she asked as she burst into tears.

"No. I'm just happy. I'm really, really happy, Mom."

She looked at me in shock and threw up her hands.

"He's dead! *Don't you understand that he's dead?*"

"I do. It's just that, now, I'm the one who feels alive. Now I can live my life the way it was supposed to be lived. Now I'm the one who can go on living."

After he died I doubted my abilities less than I had before, when I was still living in the shadow of his abuse. Getting rid of that shame set me free to pursue the one passion he tried to take from me—to leave my hometown and go to New York to live out my destiny.

Chapter
7

The Best Things in Life Are Free

After throwing away a high-paying position and moving to the biggest city in the United States, I knew I needed money, and I needed it bad. I contacted every temp agency I could, trying to get a job as fast as possible.

The agency that responded the fastest was called "Temptations." I thought the name (written in hot-pink '80s font on their website) was tacky, but beggars can't be choosers.

I put on my least-shitty clothes: a black button-down shirt and a pair of dress pants from the Gap, a place about which I once overheard a small child in the Upper East Side ask, "Mommy, don't homeless people buy clothes there?"

I hopped onto the train downtown. Everything was so exciting in New York! There was a break-dancer yelling, "Showtime!" and doing flips on the train! And then there was an odd man mumbling, "Can I ask you a question about your hair?" in Union Square! New. York. Had. It. All. The corners were filled with musicians of all stripes; no longer did I have to walk from Third and Market to Second and Market listening to a barrage of white hippies with dreads scream anti-war songs while violently strumming their guitars.

It was a bit odd that the Temptations address turned out to be an apartment building. But, not questioning this any further, I stepped inside and took the elevator to the company's floor.

I knocked on the door. Nobody answered. Gently, I turned the knob and found that it clicked open. I straightened myself up, took a breath, tried to be presentable, and held the folder of resumes close to my chest.

"I'll be there in a second!" called a female voice. I looked around. This was not a company office; it was a woman's apartment with an official-looking desk close to the door.

"The tower spells trouble for you," the woman said on the phone. "If you're not careful, you could lose a lot of money this time."

I peered around the corner and saw a middle-aged woman with a towel on her head, sitting in an office chair, wearing nothing but a bathrobe. She was holding a tarot card. When she spun around and looked at me, she held the card up to her eyeball like it was an eyepatch and smiled. I felt incredibly confused and a little creeped out at this point, but I needed the money, and my severe aversion to dick ruled out prostitution.

She hung up the phone.

"Welcome to Temptations!" she enthused wildly. "I loved your resume, and I just had to invite you in immediately. I love that you're an English major. Did you know that I was once an English major too?"

I suddenly thought of my future: alone and impoverished, would I, too, resort to fortune telling to make money? My master's in English had not proved useful in three years. In exactly one decade, I could be telling people what "The Hanged Man" really means for their broken marriages. I could be running an office out of a studio and interviewing candidates in an Egyptian-cotton bathrobe.

"That's great," I said.

"I see you've done some design work. I have the perfect job for you. There's a female-owned and -run interior design agency in midtown that needs an assistant to help them get ready for a big influx of business right before the holidays. Do you think you can do that?"

"Of course," I said. "I used to be a mid level manager for PlayStation. I can handle anything."

"Terrific," she said. "How are you with type A personalities?"

I wasn't sure at the time what that meant, so I said, "I can get along with all kinds of people!"

"Oh, thank God," she said. "I just can't get anyone to stay at this job! It pays so well, and the women are so friendly. If there's anything I can't stand, it's people who won't commit to the task at hand."

"Dedication is my middle name," I said with a shrug.

"Okay! Here's their address; you'll start tomorrow."

I ran home and called my friend back in San Francisco to tell her I'd gotten my first job in the Big Apple. Best of all, it had only taken me a day of searching.

"Esther, this sounds like a scam," she said.

"She's an artist! An English major! Hey, I believe in tarot and astrology and all that shit."

There was a pause on the line.

"Esther, it's called Temptations. Is this a real place? Are you lying to me? It sounds like a strip club. Are you out there dancing for money? Do you need help? I can send you money."

I showed up to the interior design agency at 8:45 a.m. the next day. I always try to show up at any job earlier than expected. In my head, I had dreams of a fancy interior design agency made up of lots of marble and glass. Instead, I walked into an incredibly tiny, dusty office that smelled like Raid, with four women at the helm. There were two blondes who ran the company and two brunettes who acted as an intern and an assistant. I waved hi and smiled at everyone.

The chief blonde, Ashley, came over, straightened her glasses, and appraised me thoroughly.

"I assume you know all about databases," she said.

"Well, yes, I've used Salesforce—"

"Yes, yes. Well, this is our database. We really need to send out Christmas cards to everyone on our client list. That's where you come in."

She opened a Microsoft Word document.

"This is the . . . database?" I asked. I had never heard someone refer to a plain-text Word document as if it were actual software used by businesses to track their client base.

"Yes!" she screamed. "They told me at the temp agency that you knew all about databases! Are you stupid?"

"No," I said, restraining myself.

Each day, I had to update the "database" by googling the addresses of celebrities. I'm not kidding. Regis and Kathie Lee? What better way to find their addresses than by googling them; that is surely a more accurate and dependable way to find something than actually contacting them through connections. Forget building a more realistic clientele list.

"If anyone has had a baby, *I want to know that too!*" Ashley screamed.

I spent my days stalking celebrities on the internet and trying to piece together as much information about them as possible for the "database." The other two brunettes compulsively read Perez Hilton all day and did a minimal amount of work. They cackled every time before-and-after pictures showed a pregnant celebrity packing on pounds.

Over time, I realized Ashley was abusive. She would shout, with louder and higher frequencies, that I was a complete moron each day. I worked far more than the hours for which I was being compensated. One day when I was getting ready for work, I fainted in my bathroom. I'd started my period and bled too much. I called the closest car service and spent the entire day in the hospital, hooked up to IVs.

My boss at Temptations blew up my phone the entire time I was in the hospital.

"Can't you just come in?" she demanded. "It's just a little blood. We really need that database updated."

"No, I can't," I said angrily. "I'm hemorrhaging. And my pay is late. I've only received two hundred and eighty-three dollars in pay for this entire month."

"Ugh. You *really* can't make it in today? Fine, I guess I'll be the bearer of bad news," she huffed.

I noticed that she'd said nothing about the pay.

When I came in the next day, Ashley yelled at me for going to the hospital.

"So you have some kind of supposed bleeding condition," she shouted. "Why didn't you have medicine to prevent this kind of thing from happening?"

"Well," I said, restraining my rage, "nothing like this has ever happened before. Apparently, I had an ovarian cyst that burst, and now I need to take some medicine to slow my bleeding until we figure out what to do next."

"Sure, whatever," she said. "Also, why did you turn off your computer before you left for the day?"

"You told me to turn everything off before I go home to save power."

"*No!* I specifically said *do not* turn off the computer," she screamed. "*Never* turn off the power on the database!"

I wanted to kill this woman, or at the very least hurl my excess menstrual blood all over her, *Carrie* style.

"Come. I need you to lift these books and put them on the top of this bookshelf."

"The doctor said I shouldn't lift anything heavy for two weeks so I don't bleed too much," I said.

She glared at me.

"I *said* get up on that ladder and *arrange the books at the top of this shelf.*"

I took a deep breath, gathered about five books, and then went to the top of the ladder. Over and over, she made me rearrange the books according to color, then size. I kept taking deeper breaths, trying not to pass out. Finally, I got weak and collapsed onto the bookcase. The girls who'd been watching Perez Hilton rushed over and helped me slowly get off the ladder.

"*You are useless!*" Ashley screamed. "Mop these floors! Pick up that bucket!"

She pointed to a large, industrial-sized bucket.

"That looks heavy, and I'm afraid if I can't lift five books, I probably can't lift that bucket either," I said.

"Oh, that's right," she said with a sneer. "We wouldn't want Esther to get her period and 'hurt' herself with her 'medical condition.'"

She made the boo-hoo motion under her eyes, and I said nothing before she stormed out of the room.

The three other women who worked in the office rushed over, hugged me, and asked if I was okay. They reassured me that this was part and parcel of the job, and it was not my fault.

We had about five seconds of female solidarity before Ashley came storming back into the room. She said there was a client coming in at one o'clock and that she needed a bag of ice from Duane Reade so she could serve him sparkling water. Because a free glass of water with ice in it is sure to convince any client to spend $7,000 or more.

I rushed to the nearby Duane Reade. They looked at me like I was crazy and said they'd never sold ice.

I dreaded calling Ashley again, but I wanted to make sure I did everything exactly to her specifications.

"Hi, Ashley? They don't carry ice here. Is there another place you'd prefer for me to go and get it for you?"

"*You are so stupid!*" she shouted at the top of her lungs. "Go to a fucking bodega. I don't fucking care where you get the goddamned ice. Are you a moron or something? An actual moron?"

I fought back tears. I was having the period from hell while my boss clearly had some sort of chemically imbalanced PMS that equated to forty thousand of my own cycles.

I purposefully found a filthy sack of ice in the nastiest bodega ever, hoped it would give her a disease, and trudged back to Ashley's office. She scowled at me and told me to get back to work.

I spent the next four hours googling information about Alec Baldwin et al. and then got ready to pack up and go home.

Ashley plucked a newly empty Starbucks cup from her lips and dramatically tossed it in a can.

"Take care of my trash," she commanded.

I took her trash, thinking she was garbage, hauled it down-stairs, and bit my lip until I burst out crying on the train back to Queens.

The *Confessions of a Shopaholic* album blasted in my head-phones. It made me laugh to listen to songs about fashion when my clothes were so unfashionable. I knew my-hard earned $283 could not buy designer anything.

When I got home, I polished off a bottle of wine and decided to quit the next morning. I'd come to New York to embark on the adventure of a lifetime, not to be abused by an insane designer who would have been better off using an abacus and sheepskin parchment than attempting to use a computer.

After I quit, the Temptations recruiter called, railing about how I had not seen the assignment through to completion. I apol-ogized and hung up.

Then Ashley called me; she'd gotten my personal number from the recruiter. She begged, pleaded, and cried for me to come back. She even promised to pay me double what she was paying before because, somehow in my apparent stupidity, I was the best assistant she'd ever had.

"I've received a crisp two hundred and eighty-three dollars for an entire month of work from you," I said.

"That's not my problem. That's the agency's."

"Right. But see, what is it worth to me if you pay me double of essentially nothing? I found something better, and I know my worth now."

She began to shout again, and I hung up the phone.

I hadn't really found another job. But New York was teaching me that I was worth more than nothing.

Chapter
8

Stop the Press

"A really hot New York femme power lesbian," I slurred to the bartender. I was spending my unemployed days drinking cosmos at three o'clock and drunk dialing my friends. I was worried about myself and didn't know what I needed more: a job or some ass.

"Oh, honey. Try *GRL*," he said, tossing a magazine in my direction.

My eyes became plastic balls on springs as they leaped out of my head and zoomed toward two hot girls pouting on the cover.

"Yeah, like they're gay," I said, putting my eyes back into their sockets and rolling them.

"They are. I've seen them out in the village," he said.

I wasn't sure if I'd had too many drinks or was just overwhelmed with the sheer hope that girls I wanted existed somewhere in this universe. No more angry hippies screaming at me for being "too heteronormative." This sounds ridiculous, but what I wanted was a chivalrous femme. A gentlefemme to sweep me off my feet and revive my hope in archaic romantic rituals. These girls were few and far between, but I knew they were real. Despite everything that had happened with Morgan, I knew there could be a woman out there who rocked hard femme energy and would also kiss the back of my hand. Someone else, someone who was *not* Morgan, had to exist in this world. And now I had confirmation that there was more of a chance to find her in New York City. There was hope after all!

I applied for an open editorial assistant position at GRL. I didn't think it would go anywhere because, at this point, I'd been working monotonous office jobs and applying for editorial positions since I graduated college. Each time I either heard nothing or made it to the final interview and still didn't get the job.

At one interview, I hadn't realized that I'd researched a different magazine by the same name and ended up applying for a gay men's porn magazine. Surrounded by pictures of guys going to town on glory holes and money shots on the bearded faces of leather daddies, my interviewer asked what drew me to the magazine. I mumbled something about "wanting to support the LGBT community in any possible way." But I think we both knew that I had no business typing up copy about "how to choose the right cock ring for your husband." If I were bi, I could at least give some helpful tips about dicks, but I had never handled one personally. A girl in high school once told me that penises felt like steamed turkey necks, and after nearly throwing up in my own mouth, I resolved to never be with a man, then masturbated to the twenty-seven pictures of Scary Spice hanging on my bedroom wall.

I once made it to the final interview for an internship at *Gals* magazine in San Francisco. Unfortunately, I realized my class schedule didn't line up with the publication's erratic office hours; three elder lesbians on staff gave me a hug and sent me on my way with a gift bag of lube, dental dams, and other related items.

"Where else but *Gals* can you walk in to apply for a job and leave with an entire sack of porn?" one said with a compassionate slap on my shoulder.

Ever since that brief brush with glory, I'd wanted to work for a magazine (not just for more bags of porn)—and props if it was gay. I always knew that my style wouldn't land me at a place like *Cosmo* or *ELLE*. That was for pretty, straight girls with wealthy parents from Connecticut, who went to summer camp with the boss's children. That was for good little girls with pin-straight, glossy hair and twenty tips on how to drive their boyfriends wild. That wasn't me. My destiny in life was to make zero sustainable dollars writing about pussy and crying at bars.

Could I be the gay version of that girl? Would New York welcome Esther Zinn: the dark-haired, mysterious femme mestiza with a confusingly Jewish first and last name? Could I go on a shopping spree on Park Avenue? Could I spend my days being witty at a gloriously lofty magazine by day, then walk into a lesbian bar in actual heels without falling and steal every lady's attention by night? It could happen! Anything could happen in the Big Apple. Days later, I unexpectedly received a phone call asking me to come in for an interview and was hired on the spot.

I envisioned a polished office of ivory and marble, like you see in every movie about a single girl living in New York. No one ever tells you that every single magazine and publishing house in New York looks like an accountant's office from 1973.

I arrived a bit early on my first day, and no one was there to let me in. So I stood outside for about forty-five minutes until a cute, dark-haired Italian butch arrived and said, "Oh! I'm sorry about that! You're the new girl, aren't you?"

"Yes, I am. Did I arrive too early?"

"No, you came at the right time. It's just that everybody has hangovers," she said, opening the door.

Inside, the office was a modest, single room with a handful of computers. It didn't look the way I'd envisioned based on movies, but it wasn't too different from the *Gals* office.

I awkwardly checked my phone (for nothing) and tried to look busy. My new coworkers shuffled in around eleven o'clock.

There was Colette, the six-foot-tall Romanian (and my new boss). There was Kathy, a heterosexual blonde saleswoman who used to work for Condé Nast. There was Angelina, a freckled and bitter woman with cold gray eyes who often boasted about coming from a powerful family in the Mafia. And finally, there was Beaux, who had let me in. She had close-cropped hair, strong shoulders, full red lips, and an easygoing smile. It was very rare for me to feel even a spark of attraction to women who were not high maintenance, wildly unfaithful femmes—so femme they bordered on looking straight. Part of Morgan's mysterious allure had been that she didn't look gay or straight but like some kind of impossible, charming mermaid who dwelled deep in the oceans of a planet that was not even Earth. Everyone told me I should have expected some mystery about her to knock me on my ass for this very reason, but I couldn't help being drawn to her like a moth to the flame. She was exactly my type, a type I couldn't even articulate properly when trying to describe her to other people.

Still, I looked at Beaux as something curious and fun, like trying exotic fusion cuisine for the first time after a lifetime of Jimmy Dean's breakfast sandwiches. Oh, if ever I were to go butch! I would devour her very soul all night long, and nothing would be left afterward but a heap of ashes and the scent of Drakkar Noir.

Once Beaux came in late after a date, and she was carrying an entire backpack of dildos. She'd stayed up all night screwing some model from Miami in a hotel. I wondered what the entire backpack was used for. Beaux worked in distribution. Anytime someone made a joke about porn and pizza delivery men, I wondered what it would be like to have Beaux randomly deliver an entire box of magazines to my doorstep and then to pull her into the threshold by her necktie (I don't think she ever wore a necktie—that was part of the fantasy).

Over the next few months, my enthusiasm about finding love in New York was more or less snuffed out. My coworkers were chronically tired and always upset over a breakup. It was not unusual for someone to come in at one o'clock crying about an unfaithful ex or unclear relationship boundaries. Just hearing that made me never want to try again after loving and losing Morgan. I quickly resolved to become a gay nun.

It was 2010, and everybody smoked like we were still living in the seventies. I was quiet as I did my work and everybody thought I was weird.

Kathy shared stories about men. At one point she screamed, "How will I ever get some dick in this town when all day long I'm surrounded by *lesbians, lesbians, lesbians*!" Angelina seemed constantly annoyed and would blast terrible music out of her computer at top volume, with no consideration for anyone but herself. Colette was a yes woman who went along with whatever Angelina wanted. I once asked her why she did everything Angelina said. She gave me a fearful look and whispered conspiratorially, "You have *no idea* what power she wields in the lesbian scene." I thought that was ridiculous.

More or less, I kept to myself and tried to do my assignments on my own. Though I hearted NY women, I was too shy and fearful to hit on anybody. The lesbian scene consists of twenty-five to fifty people who all talk no matter what city you're in, so I was cautious. It's truly like *Game of Thrones* no matter where you go: five small groups of lesbians vying for power, and people being executed for their betrayals or inability to fit in.

My first assignment was to write a Valentine's Day gift guide pointing lesbians toward the perfect presents for their girlfriends. While working on it, I'd occasionally tear up thinking about Morgan, but I never shared the details of my sordid and mysterious past with my coworkers. The long list I created included everything from activity dates to luxury sex toys to a set of ceramic earrings that looked like two matching, smiling slices of bread with peanut butter and jelly on them.

The earrings got cut.

It was now a few months since I'd moved. A friend of mine called to ask if I was being glamorous, buying designer shoes, and going on a ton of dates like all the girls on TV who move to New York. I said I wasn't over Morgan yet, so I spent most Friday nights hanging out with an elderly woman on the first floor of my apartment building who'd just lost her husband of fifty years. She said, "You're doing New York all wrong—call me when it gets interesting" and hung up.

I know for a fact that I bored the girls, because I barely spoke. Who would want to work with a mute? Instead of having me continue to write daily news articles, they began to send me on distribution runs with Beaux.

We drove all over the city, bringing magazines to drop boxes while Beaux shared stories about an insane woman who constantly abused her emotionally. Once, she cried. I hugged her while we sat parked in a random area in the Bronx, and for the life of me, I could not understand who would be idiotic enough to be so careless with such a beautiful butch.

At one point, we had to drive all the way outside the city to drop off surplus magazines at a storage unit. Beaux lifted gigantic boxes with her rippling muscles and deposited them into the unit while I helplessly lifted—at best—half a box, trying not to trip and fall in heels and a dress. Afterward, Beaux and I laughed at how hilariously useless I was, then went to a McDonald's to have a quick lunch before heading back to the office. Suddenly, she started to giggle. It became contagious. So we were laughing deliriously.

"What's so funny? Why are you laughing? I'm just laughing because you're laughing," I said.

"It's this. That we spent all day at that storage facility, and you were too worried about chipping your nails. That we're in a McDonald's. And it's not just a McDonald's—it's a McDonald's *in* Jersey. It's *our lives!*"

On the long drive back, I smiled wide and looked out at the city lights.

We walked back to the office, and Angelina was outside smoking and talking on the phone. "Have the money for me by five o'clock, dickbag!" she screamed.

I went inside, got my purse, and got on the train back to Queens. Although I was excited to work for a queer magazine, doing distribution wasn't my life's dream, even if I got to use that time to ogle Beaux's muscles. I wondered if it was time to leave *GRL* and find another opportunity.

Later that night, I got a call from work. It was the elusive, mysterious editor-in-chief with an invitation to join her at her penthouse for an exclusive party at the end of the week.

When The Chief spoke, you listened.

Chapter
9

The Red-Light Special

The Chief fascinated me. We were about the same height (a whopping five feet two), yet she loomed larger than life. The Chief was a classic New Yorker who never slept and was almost always chain smoking; she was a perfectionist who didn't suffer fools or mistakes gladly (to the point of screaming, *"I hate my liiiiiiiiife!"* at the top of her lungs if she discovered a small error in the copy postproduction). She often crucified herself with the same self-deprecating humor that I had. The Chief wore her short, curly hair underneath a baseball cap that I never once saw her take off. She often called herself "the lesbian Danny DeVito," but I never thought that was true; I thought she didn't give herself enough credit.

Sometimes I look at people and feel like I can see their past lives—or, at the very least, I can see into a time in their lives where something major happened to turn them into who they are. When I looked at the Chief, I saw a tomboy dyke who'd charmed many a lady and broken her fair share of hearts. She was older than me and lived with a lover who, for all intents and purposes, was her wife. Still, that party girl glimmered through. That part of her hadn't disappeared when she reached her fifties.

Blessed with an abnormal amount of charisma, she had a youthful and impish smile and could talk anyone in or out of anything. The Chief could call you up at three o'clock in the morning to edit something down to the wire—and you would most likely do it because why not? It was for the Chief. If the lesbian scene was like *Game of Thrones*, then the Chief was like Varys with his little birds; within fifteen minutes of anything happening in or around the Village, the Chief would know about it. Once I went on a date, and the Chief called me about it as soon as I woke up hours later.

"What happened? Did you have a good time? I heard you two were quite the fixture!"

To this day, I have no idea how she knew where/when/who I was with, but she knew it all. The Chief was the undisputed kingpin of lesbian nightlife. Once, she told me to please stop calling her "the Chief" and insisted I call her "Big Boss Lady." I said, "Okay, Chief."

When she first invited me to her house, all she mentioned was that the party was for some of the city's top sex bloggers. Apparently, a dildo company from overseas wanted to advertise in the magazine, so we had to be on our best behavior. I didn't know what her place would be like. The Chief's place turned out to be an elegant penthouse in the Upper West Side with a balcony that overlooked the city.

"Let's get to work and get these ladies some booze!" she said when I arrived. I was ready to work as an impromptu coat-check girl and bartender.

Throughout the night, impossibly pretty girls in tasteful black cocktail dresses would come by and ask for glasses of merlot. I wasn't surprised that they were all femme sex bloggers—anybody that hot was certainly worth writing home about. Occasionally, I snuck sips for myself so I wouldn't be nervous about the human contact. Although I was more or less a party girl, I was never quite comfortable in crowds unless I had enough drinks to forget about my potential to make an ass of myself purely by existing.

Suddenly, I heard cheers coming from the front door. Zoe, a punky butch with a faux-hawk, had arrived. I took her leather jacket and placed it in the closet.

She was an excitable storyteller and snagged the eyes of many girls at the party as she made wild gestures and told jokes. I watched them all look her way throughout the night, and I wondered what somebody had to do to be noticed by a gorgeous girl like that. Eventually, I went over and talked with her for a bit, hoping to suss out the secret behind her magnetism. We learned as we chatted that we were both biracial. She was Korean and German, and I related to her, being Filipino and German.

I felt perhaps some of the doting directed my way was done out of pity. Zoe was extremely good looking—I, however, tended to rely on my "charm" and the expedient convenience of my wanton ways to consistently get either 0 percent ass or far too much. My face was sexy-ugly, and I always knew that. Part of why I frequently got so drunk was so that I could be witty enough to be smooth. My therapist later diagnosed me with facial dysmorphia, which I contested was just a healthy case of "tellin' it like it is."

Across the room, I saw a dark-haired beauty with giant, cat-eyed glasses and a perfect pout. She was writing in a notebook. She had full lips the color of raspberries and wore fishnets that accented the tattoos covering her legs. I smiled at her a couple of times, and she smiled back. I thought she was just being polite.

"Zoe? I have a question," I said. "How do you get so many girls? Everyone here has made eyes at you all night."

"You just have to be confident," she said. She might as well have told me that water was wet.

"I like that girl. That one over there reading. I don't know what to say or how to be cool. I just . . . don't know."

"Just say hello. Give it a shot."

The Chief walked up behind me then, having overheard the last part of the conversation.

"Oh, she's cute! That one's perfect for you. Go for it! I'm rooting for ya! You've just gotta do it."

The Chief slapped me on the back, and I decided to take a deep breath and approach. I said hello to the dark-haired beauty and asked her for her name. She said her name was Victoria.

"Victoria . . . that name is so pretty and mysterious," I said, trying to flirt. "Nothing else here seems to hold your attention tonight. What are you writing in that notebook?"

"I'm working on a memoir," she said.

"What's it about?"

"I'm an escort," she said. She smirked and took a sip of red wine from her glass.

"That's . . . cool!" I said, not knowing how else to respond. I excused myself and went to find the Chief slicing up hors d'oeuvres in the kitchen.

"God damn it, Chief," I whispered, angrily. "She's a prostitute!"

"She was? Ha!" The Chief cackled as she continued to slice cheese. "Well she's very good looking, I guess you have expensive taste."

"Did you know? Why would you try to set me up with her?

I'm not *that* desperate." I wasn't making value judgments about this woman, but I felt that a value judgment had been made about me; that I was so pathetically obsessed with not getting over Morgan that people thought I had no choice but to pay to get some ass.

"Oh stop being such a prude. It's a respectable profession, like any other. Think of it as picking up extra shifts at Old Navy during the holidays. They are *healthcare providers*. Do you know how much better off lesbians would be if they didn't U-Haul with the first pretty young thing that crosses their paths?"

"I don't know why you would do this to me!" I shouted.

"Honey, you said you wanted a well-read woman. You didn't say she couldn't be a hooker."

Zoe walked into the end of the conversation.

"Did I just hear that she's a call girl?"

"Yes," I grumbled, boiling over with shame.

"Innnnteresting," Zoe said. She popped a grape into her mouth and walked over to Victoria, putting her arm around her. Every now and then, I'd look over to see Victoria giggling at Zoe's jokes.

Very quickly, Zoe sealed the deal and went home with her.

I walked back behind the bar and continued to pour drinks only for myself, wondering if it was weird to be a poor loser over a girl I wasn't interested in. Whenever someone asked for a glass, I simply handed them the bottle. My lips ran dark with merlot, as though I'd just swallowed entire mouthfuls of blood.

I went to the edge of the terrace and looked at the million little lights.

The Chief tapped me on the shoulder. "I thought you left already. What are you thinking?"

"I'm thinking that I'm upset you cut my ceramic peanut butter and jelly earrings from the Valentine's Day gift guide. They were so cute."

"They were the ugliest things I'd ever seen," the Chief said.

"The bread slices were a perfect match for each other! Soulmates!"

"God. I will buy you those earrings if you never mention them again, and we can put this whole thing behind us," the Chief said. "I'm sure they cost five dollars at some hipster swap meet."

"Okay, fine. I wasn't thinking about the earrings. I was thinking about how odd it is to be in a city so large yet feel so alone. Each of these tiny lights represents a little home with strangers I may or may not ever meet. It's just fascinating, I think."

"Where do you live?" the Chief asked.

"Astoria."

She laughed at me. "Did the broker tell you 'It's the new Williamsburg?' They've been telling people that for at least ten years. Any roommates?"

"Nah, just me and the cat."

The Chief looked at me somewhat sadly, as though registering something and filing it away.

"Get home safe, honey," she said.

I finished my drink, grabbed my jacket, and headed out to get a taxi. As I rode home, the car sped over the Queensboro Bridge. It was just the first of what would be perhaps hundreds of late nights when I'd make this trip with my head spinning, my heart longing, as I stared at all the lights over the water.

Chapter
10

Hail to the Chief

The Chief asked me to come over again not long after the party. It wasn't uncommon for her to hold weeklong editorial marathon sessions at a smaller guest apartment she had downtown. Every month, various members of the staff would come by on a rotating basis to essentially live there as we hunted for errors, checked facts, drank copious amounts of coffee, and frequently passed out on the Chief's floor. I don't think I ever saw the Chief go to bed, not even once during those weeks. I remember living in awe of her dedication to the magazine and, at the same time, worrying deeply about her health. She'd found a way to change and influence the world with just her words. I wondered if it might be too late for me to find my own way to do this in life.

During one of these weeks, the Chief and I were the only ones left after the other staff members went home in desperate need of sleep. The Chief had been taking occasional breaks that she spent compulsively watching her favorite TV show on the Oxygen Channel, *Snapped*, which is about female felons who committed murder. I privately wondered what this said about the Chief's taste in women.

She'd called me up at one o'clock in the morning that night and asked me to bring over as much caffeine as possible. I was an actual caffeine junkie and had caffeinated soap, caffeinated hot chocolate, caffeinated marshmallows, and caffeinated cookies that I'd purchased from a shady-looking site online. I frequently wondered whether these things were legal, then I decided that they had to be since they had official-looking nutritional facts on the box. Everyone in New York had some kind of vice; I figured I was allowed to blindly drink five or more appletinis a night and eat marshmallows with 250 milligrams of caffeine in them as long as I never tried coke or heroin.

So I made caffeinated mint hot chocolate in her kitchen at three o'clock in the morning and topped it with a marshmallow, creating a drink that was the caffeine equivalent of five coffees. After preparing two mugs in the same fashion as someone might boil illicit substances over a stove, I brought them over to the Chief. She took a sip and made a face.

"Too sweet! This tastes terrible. You actually drink this stuff?"

"Yes! I love it," I said, my eyes bugging out and my heart racing. "Five coffees. One mug. Five coffees."

"Ugh, God, I can't have any more of this. Let's go drive and get some real coffee."

We got into the Chief's car, and I wondered how a born-and-bred city girl could ever drive. She said it was meditative, that it helped her clear her head. I'd never learned to drive. At one point I had my permit, but I failed the driver's test all three times. I often joked to people that my 50 percent Asian side had a 50 percent chance of killing everybody on the road.

"So how goes the dating, kiddo?" she asked as she drove.

"Eh, not fantastic," I said with a sigh, popping another caffeinated marshmallow into my mouth.

The Chief looked concerned. "What's the latest?"

"I don't know. A few months ago I went on a few dates with a closeted Muslim. She wasn't ready to come out to anybody and was married to some D-level movie star in Afghanistan. She also said I should be ashamed to march in Pride and that she would 'bash my brains into the sidewalk' if I stopped seeing her. After that, I decided to essentially never try again and just pine after Morgan for the rest of my life."

"Honey, I'm guessing there were some red flags here that you ignored," the Chief said. "Also, please stop crying over that girl. We don't know how much of what she told you was the truth and how much was false. The next time you cry over her, just think of her giving a hand job to her little boyfriend. Or was he her husband? Whatever. Think of her giving it to him real hard!"

A wet marshmallow fell out of my mouth and onto my lap.

"I want to die thinking of that, Chief. I want to fucking die."

"Yeah, well, you will die if you don't get over her. Or I will if I have to hear about her again. Anyway, the other girl. Red flags. What were they?"

"Yeah, the first was when she gave me the 'New York Experience.'"

We rolled to a red light, and the Chief turned to stare at me, befuddled.

"And what would that be?"

"Ugh, I don't know! She told me that she was a real New York native, that she would show me all the sights you don't normally see in the guidebooks. She said, 'Babe, I'll give you the whole New York Experience.' I thought maybe we'd go to some hole-in-the-wall pizzeria and see a cool underground band. Instead, she led me around the corner of the Cubbyhole, and we sat in an actual gutter. I said, 'What are we doing?' She said,

'This. This is it. We can do so much people watching from here. What more could you ask for? This is New York; it's all around us. This is the New York Experience.' She held my hand, and everything smelled like garbage."

The Chief blinked, then suddenly burst out laughing. I kept waiting for her to stop, but she clenched the steering wheel, shaking with chuckles until tears formed in her eyes.

"My God! This is hilarious!" she cried.

"It didn't really feel all that funny when it happened," I said.

"I'm glad I'm getting to know you better," the Chief said. "You're really funny! We can't let this go to waste. We just can't. Let's use your powers for good. We'll give you a column. Yes! Your own column—that's it. Like Carrie Bradshaw, but for lesbians. We'll make it a play on *Sex and the City*. I've got it! Broads in the Big Apple!"

"I'm not the lesbian Carrie Bradshaw," I said. "And I don't really go on a lot of dates. This is crazy."

"It's just crazy enough that it could work."

"Crazy enough that what could work?"

"Me getting you laid!" she yelled, victoriously. "By the power vested in me, we *will* get you laid! You'll have so many girls banging down your door that you won't know what to do with all of them. Ha!"

She slapped the steering wheel resolutely, satisfied with her brilliant plan. I folded my arms and smiled, excited to see my name in lights and also thoroughly confused by how I could be any kind of sex or dating expert when I was the exact opposite of that. How could I tell people how to be happy in their love lives when I didn't have one and potentially could never have one again? Though I'd had no complaints in the bedroom, and my first girlfriend embarrassingly posted in a public lesbian forum that I was indeed "the best sex she'd ever had," I certainly did not see myself pulling off some kind of crazy, acrobatic maneuver in bed that would leave everybody hanging on my every word. I thought about all the crazy advice I'd read in *Cosmo*. "Simply stand on your head and spin your pelvis around 360 degrees! That will really turn your boyfriend on."

We eventually rolled up to a bodega. I ordered a black coffee for the Chief and got a ninety-nine-cent lemon pie for myself. Then I hopped back into the car and handed her the cup.

"Just trust me on this one," she said, grinning. She took a long, deep sip of the coffee and sighed. "Now this is the real stuff. Not that crazy marshmallow shit!"

I thought to myself, *I can't do this. But maybe I should try. Nothing terrible can happen that hasn't already happened to me at least three times.*

"Why did we drive all this way?" I asked. "We got into a car for possibly Folgers coffee that we could have gotten at an identical bodega near the apartment."

"I just wanted to drive longer," the Chief said. "Plus only real New Yorkers know which places are worth getting coffee from in the middle of the night. Now that's the New York Experience. Wouldn't you agree?"

Chapter
11

Broads in the Big Apple

I continued to write my column, Broads in the Big Apple. It briefly became comic relief for a microscopic subset of lesbian magazine journalists in the city—a bit of an inside joke for them to use their influence to find me a date. When New Yorkers commit to something, they make it a team effort. A reporter from *Time Out* magazine dubbed me, "One of New York's City's Most Eligible Lesbian Bachelorettes" of 2011, which was funny because there were maybe ten eligible lesbian bachelorettes in the entire city, so it wasn't that lofty of an accomplishment.

Whenever I'd go out to bars, people recognized me from my column. Girls would ask me for advice on their relationships. How could they get their ex-girlfriend to come back? How could they know if their current girlfriend was cheating? And how could I tell these people that I'd been broken by a woman who'd secretly married a man, that I was so horribly incapable of getting any ass that the Chief gave me a dating column out of pity?

I no longer worked in the office at this point—in case you weren't aware, lesbian journalism isn't a huge moneymaker, so I spent most of my time at a communal workspace for writers below 14th Street, attempting to freelance articles and design websites for clients who gave helpful directions such as, "Make it orange. I want all of it to be orange."

Every week I would call up the magazine and tell the web editor when I'd uploaded my latest story. She was new, and I'd never met her in person. I had no idea what she looked like. She was a husky, sensual, disembodied voice on a landline, and she sounded like a phone-sex operator.

Every time she answered the phone, she'd say, "Hello, Juliet speaking," and I'd feel like I was having a heart attack, panic, and just hang up. I was now a twenty-nine-year-old woman, and the sheer sex appeal of her voice made me feel like a child afraid to call Domino's and order a pizza from an adult. I would have to wait fifteen minutes to call back, and then I'd stammer, "Hello, my piece is up, goodbye" and just hang up again.

Every week, I dreaded calling Juliet and sounding like an idiot. Once, I called just to hear her say, "I hope your piece is ready for me. I need it in really badly," and I just hung up the phone without saying anything.

A few days after I submitted my article, she wrote me a message asking if I'd like to go for drinks sometime. I already had a date lined up, but I canceled it because I was too curious about what Juliet was like in person. I figured, *Why not? Now I can finally see the person behind this voice.*

When I walked into the bar, I was met with an olive-skinned, golden-haired femme with deep-blue eyes who was wearing a tight black cocktail dress. There was something paradoxical about her—she carried herself in a showy, confident way that also betrayed a delicate and smoldering grace. Everything about her body language said, "Come hither, but not unbidden." Her eyes had a queenly, even gaze, knowing and sad.

I found her stunning, and this was perplexing to me. I had grown up around blonde-haired family members bad-mouthing my Filipino mother for being a gold digger, totally overlooking the fact that my father was a diagnosed sociopath who'd bought a human being out of a catalog. I only ever equated blondes with racism.

Our eyes locked, and she smirked; her impish grin was contagious, and soon, I smiled too. We spent the night talking about our favorite books. She loved writers like Dostoevsky, which was intimidating.

"What are some of your favorite books?" she asked.

"I love Ann Bannon. Laura Landon in *Odd Girl Out* is my favorite character. When I was first coming out, I read about Laura finding herself, moving to New York, and going on so many adventures in search of love with other glamorous city girls. When I finished the book, I knew that someday I would go to New York and search for love too."

"Oh?" she said, intrigued. "I wouldn't have pegged you for a lover of 1950s romance. Still, I felt the same way when I was a teenager. I knew after reading Bannon that there was something for me too."

My heart tumbled a bit; it was the second time in my entire life that I met anyone familiar with Ann Bannon. The only other girl who'd read Bannon was Morgan. I hadn't felt such an instant attraction to someone since that fateful weekend in Chicago. For two years, I felt mostly empty, experiencing only tiny sparks of attraction that quickly fizzled out. Now, I couldn't stop staring at this magical new stranger who'd surprised me out of nowhere; a girl who knew all about my favorite romance novels and looked like she'd stepped out of one. I searched her eyes and thought, *Will you be a new friend—or maybe a little more? Can I know you tonight?*

"I need to ask you some questions," she said. "First of all, why do you keep drinking cosmos? Is that a part of your character?"

"Well, I don't know," I said. "That's what everyone drinks in New York on TV, right?"

She laughed. "Fair enough." Then she ordered two more cosmos.

"Okay, I need to ask you something else," she said. "Why do you keep calling me about your assignments and hanging up?"

"I don't know what you're talking about," I said, looking away awkwardly.

"Oh, Esther." She sighed. "Did it ever occur to you that we have caller ID at the magazine?"

My face ran hot with embarrassment, heart pounding. She looked at me and flashed that impish smirk, tossed her hair over her shoulder, then burst out laughing.

"Your voice scares me," I said.

"It frightens you? I sound scary?"

"No, you just sounded really hot, and I found it alarming."

She laughed. "Up until now, I only ever thought of you as the freelance writer with really awkward phone skills. And I thought your stories were hilarious. Every time I edited them, I kept thinking about how I wanted to meet you and make a new friend."

The jig was up, game set and match. There were now eleven cosmos sitting on the table. Feeling somewhat bold, I leaned back and put my arm around her.

"Oh. Do friends do that?" she asked.

She gave me a soft and smoldering kiss that sent a shiver through my body.

In the same voice that had chided me for comma splices over

the phone, she whispered, "Do friends do this?" as the tips of her hair gently grazed my collarbone.

I didn't say anything back, just returned her affections with a fiery volley of kisses. There were so many things I wanted to tell her and couldn't. Then she whispered, "I love the way you kiss; I haven't felt a kiss like that in so very long. It's been so many years."

She'd said exactly what I was thinking; I had long haunted gay bars on both sides of the country, and I'd kissed so many lovers that I'd forgotten most of their names. By the time I was twenty-three, I had kissed perhaps sixty or seventy women. Many times, I tasted sadness on their lips, but more often than not, I tasted nothing. I tried to think back, past some faces that I remembered and others that were just outlines. What did a kiss taste like? I'd forgotten and felt them only as one would experience a phantom limb.

Her kiss tasted like something. The tiny little zap that I felt inside became an electric volt.

"Look at the time," I said, pulling away and trying to catch my breath. It was three o'clock in the morning. "I have to get home."

"Of course. You might get in trouble with your boss if you don't submit tomorrow," she said with a grin.

I started to panic, thinking about the full weight of what had just happened. The electric volt kiss that made it hard to walk. So I gave her an awkward hug and ran away as fast as possible, diving into a taxi like I was starring in an action movie.

My phone buzzed.

She'd texted, "So. Are we dating now?"

I texted back. "Hmm. Dating already? After just a kiss? What kind of girl do you take me for?"

"After that kiss, I think I have just a little idea of what kind of girl to take you for."

A week later, we decided to go on another date.

"I think we should get in our finest outfits. And go bowling," I said.

"Well. Bowling is quite the blue-collar sport. This is absurd. So we should probably do this tonight."

She showed up later that evening in a black suit, and I showed up in a black dress. I told her she looked like an anchorwoman. She said, "You look like a weather girl. At least I report the hard news."

I observed her mannerisms and her speech, noticing she'd had a few before coming to meet me. Not coincidentally, I had too (because the actual terror of being around her still made me want to throw up).

"Do you know how to bowl?"

"No, not really," I said. "Actually, I kind of suck at it. But I love bowling because it's the one sport nobody looks cool doing, and there is literally no physical benefit to doing it."

She laughed and we drank umpteen cosmos at the bowling alley's bar, trying hard to be "ironic." And then we hit the lanes.

"Excuse me," she said, approaching a straight couple. "My girlfriend and I are from a professional bowling league in Iowa, and we need someone who's a *real* challenge. Would you play us in a match?"

The couple agreed. At this point we'd had maybe six or seven drinks apiece, and every time we went to throw a ball, it didn't end up anywhere except the gutter.

"Are you two really in a bowling league?" the woman asked.

"We're the best in Iowa!" Juliet said.

"We've gotta get out of here," I whispered. "I'm so drunk that this is bordering between hilarious and absurd."

"Let's break into the movie theater and make out during a movie, then sneak into another movie when we get bored. Until we make out through every movie playing," she whispered back.

I thought about it. Could someone be arrested for sneaking into a movie theater? Hot.

We ran in through a side door and kept cycling through the screenings. I wasn't sure how many were in this theater. My thoughts were running wild. *This place is a veritable labyrinth. Well, she is a good kisser. Am I breaking the law? I hope so.*

Finally, we made it to the last movie.

"Mom? I have cancer," the actor said on-screen.

"This is killing my buzz," I slurred. "I can't make out to this."

"Come home with me then," she said, shrugging. "It's me or cancer."

I tapped my lip and paused, trying to decide.

"Don't think about it. Just do it. When was the last time you did something without thinking? I already know you want to."

Before I could answer, she pushed me into a random cab on the corner and gave the driver her address.

"See? You made the right choice," she said.

My heart felt as if it were about to burst. *I made it here*, I thought. *I'm making out with a magazine editor in a taxi in New York City. This is a movie; this is a movie.*"

We entered her dark apartment, and like the lusty protagonist in any romance novel, she tried to throw me down on her bed. We missed and fell onto the floor in a fit of passion. Jonathan Franzen and David Foster Wallace novels came crashing down around my head. She breathed into my ear, "If you love lowbrow trashy romance novels so much, then I will rip your bodice off. Let me rip your bodice off you tonight." Then she actually did rip my bra apart.

"Whoa," she said, looking down. "You're pierced there?"

I shrugged.

She tore off my underwear and felt between my legs.

"You're pierced *there*?"

I shrugged again.

"I've never been with a girl that's pierced like that. What if I fuck it up, accidentally rip off your clit and maim you?"

"Uh . . . don't," I said.

If Juliet were an element, she'd be air, for she was like an unpredictable cyclone. A gentle, playful breeze that started to caress softly, then gradually whirled about, circling me up fast and hard into the sky. I never once worried about crashing down afterward; all I could do in the moment was suspend my disbelief and focus on how exciting it was to temporarily fly.

We spent six hours with our limbs intertwined, panting and whispering adorations of praise as our hands remained locked in each other's hair. Then we fell asleep for an hour or so and went back at it for three more hours. I remember thinking that at least several times a year, young teenage men in their prime die from playing online RPGs for forty-eight hours straight. If a person can die from two days of sedentary activity, could I die from this much sex with my editor?

I had a voracious appetite for her, maybe because I'd starved myself for too long from real physical affection. Soon it was already afternoon. Then I asked where her strap-ons were.

"You want *strap-ons*?" she cried, slapping her hand to her forehead.

"Yeah . . . why?"

"Those are kind of an all-day affair, hon. They're a real big production. I don't know. I don't know if I have the energy for that." She fell back in bed, flummoxed. But as she fell, she grabbed me around the waist and kissed me everywhere. She matched my ferocious appetite for passion, equal parts romantic and equal parts dirty. That ratio is hard to get wrong.

From then on, we spent about 98 percent of our days sexting, starting when we woke up until maybe five or six o'clock, when she'd rush home from work and then call me so we could either have phone sex or watch porn together. I don't know how we never ran out of stuff to say to each other; you'd think at some point we would have. I mean, you can only tell another human being how badly you want to fuck them so many times. Still, months passed, and not only did our dirty talk not decrease—it actually increased.

There was complexity in her seduction. I think she was the chattiest lover I ever had. Dirty talk is half of what gets me off. Sometimes we would treat each other like goddesses, panting and worshiping the impossible beauty of each other's eyes, lips, hair. Other times, we taunted and jousted with insults to make the other come.

"You're a debased slut with the wettest pussy. I bet you'll get wet for anyone, yet you're begging to be filled up only by me," she whispered.

"Oh? Well you're a worthless whore who should feel ashamed to work in media because your mouth is only good enough to be used."

Sometimes we got so terribly vicious with each other that it made one or both of us laugh but would then provoke the other into a few more hours of sex—out of anger or horniness, I can't really say. Maybe I should have talked it out in therapy.

Sometimes our caresses were gentle and intimate. Other times, our fingers were gnarled into fistfuls of each other's hair as if we were locked in battle, trying to kill each other. Once she yanked my hair hard as we locked eyes, stroking me rough and full against my G-spot.

"Ah, you're being so good," she purred. "On your back, with your legs wide open, just for me. So hot. Show me how good you can be."

Hmm, I thought. *I think this is the first time I've been praised for literally doing nothing in bed but existing. Lay like this? Fine.*

Once when we were on a moonlit walk, I threw her up against a wall and kissed her hard. She laughed, then somehow escaped my grip and threw *me* up against the wall, pulling my hair and whispering not-so-sweet nothings as she shoved her hand down my pants in public. We fucked in an alley. She really did not care.

When we fucked, we did it desperately, as if to confirm the other was real. When I tasted her, I sucked on her gently, and she pushed my head down. I wondered if this was how straight women felt giving head to noncommittal guys they secretly loved and could never have. So hot. When she came, she tried to push my head away, but I grabbed her hands and pinned them under her. I followed her rhythm, giving her more flat and steady licks to make her shake, and I said, "You'll finish coming when I tell you that I've had enough. And I haven't; I could fuck you every night and every day and always want more of you."

It was the first time in ages I didn't have to fake or exaggerate anything. Our sex was like an Apple product: it just worked. And it was also like Steve Jobs giving a keynote: just when you thought it was over and there couldn't possibly be anything else to consider, there was always *one more thing.*

What I loved more than anything was to be filled up by her; so often did lesbians miss my G-spot that I wondered how straight women got by. She was the only person other than Morgan to understand how I wanted to be fucked. Each time she'd stroke against that exact spot, and once she ever-so-arrogantly whispered, "I know what that pussy wants and what it needs. I know where to hit you, babe."

I despised nothing more than the embarrassment of having to admit it was true.

She often knew what I wanted without me even saying it. The first time we were together, she fucked me into an actual stupor, and all I could do was pant, "Please." It could have meant anything. She nodded and understood. Maybe that's why she was in the business of editing—she had a gift for helping inept writers like me figure out what we were trying to say, in and out of bed.

Although Juliet always seemed to intuitively know these things, she did once accidentally fuck me in the ass. I didn't say anything in the moment. It was my birthday, and I was incredibly stoned, so I was thinking about how everything is connected in the universe. She admitted afterward that she hadn't realized what she was doing until it was too late.

"I don't know what's funnier: that you accidentally mistook the service door for the VIP entrance—or that I was so high I let you," I said.

"Well, I love ass sex, but I guess I didn't consider whether or not you did," she quipped.

"I love spending time with you. Let's keep doing this," I panted. "Well, maybe not *that*."

Chapter
12

Friends Without Benefits

After about a month, Juliet and I decided to go on a date to the opera. She kept asking me to wear a tie, and I thought that was somewhat silly, but I found a red necktie and put it on.

She was the most beautiful girl I'd ever seen. Dark lashes, as smoky as her breathy voice. Eyes like seawater at high tide that signaled something more, impending danger. I sat across from the door of an Italian restaurant in Brooklyn as she stepped in wearing a black, form fitting cocktail dress that hugged her olive skin. The parts of her that were German were so . . . Germanic. Yet hints of that Italian side betrayed her in her tan skin, her every curve.

This time, she was the one in a black dress, and I was the one in a black suit.

She searched for a beat, looking for me, and I thought that perhaps I wanted her to keep trying so I could behold her longer in that easy grace, in a moment of quiet pause that stirred my heart into a tempest. I wasn't the only person who stared—the waiters stopped what they were doing and looked on. I wondered what it felt like to walk into a room and be so adored, so worshiped, with no effort. Did she even know the effect she had on others? She bore an arrogance and an elegance when she spoke, punctuating her points with the flick of a cigarette balanced between the tips of her fingers. Yet she sometimes carried herself so self-consciously. She knew that she was clever, that she was desired. Yet the part of her that secretly signaled, "Please don't make fun of me for this" was so apparent to me.

Those blue eyes lit up.

"Ah! There you are."

I stood, gave her a small kiss, and pulled out her chair.

"So fancy," she said with a smirk. "You wore the tie."

"You're the only person who could get me to do this," I said. "Do I look like a big bull dyke to you?"

"*Yes*," she said, fake swooning. "You are just so big and tough and *so* butch. I can hardly believe your swagger. It goes really well with your sparkly eyeshadow. Let's get an appetizer, please? I'm so hungry; I drove all the way out here to Brooklyn, and I'm starving."

"That's a long drive," I said, only half-heartedly scanning the menu. "Why did you take your car?"

"I thought it might be nice. Who wants to get onto the subway after something so glamorous? You'll have to forgive that my car is essentially shit, but, well, your carriage awaits, madame."

I burst out laughing. "I forgot to tell you: I find ordinary suburban things like cars oh-so-very exotic."

She said, "I can drive a stick, you know. Are you into chicks with sticks?"

"Well, I love a girl who can drive. Since I'm half Asian with no driver's license, do you think there's a 50 percent chance my driving could kill everybody on the road?"

She burst out laughing.

A waiter approached, his retinas practically swan diving into her cleavage.

"Can I start you off with anything?"

"Ah, yes," she said. "Aspic! Thanks."

She blushed a little.

"I get the impression that you aren't quite sure what you ordered," I said.

The blush deepened. Then she frowned, her grand pride wounded.

"You clearly didn't know what it was either, by the look of things!"

"I do not. Look at us. Two plebs attempting a romantic date at the opera."

"Hot."

The waiter returned with our order, gently setting a plate of meat and gelatin and two glasses of wine on the table.

"What the fuck did I just order, if you'll pardon my French. This looks like goddamned cat food," she said.

We both burst out laughing and picked at what we decided was horrible.

"Maybe this isn't our style," I said. "Should we go back to the McDonald's near your house and order two Filet-O-Fish sandwiches?"

Juliet rolled her eyes.

"Or we could always put this into a tiny bag and feed it to our cats."

"Yes. There's nothing classier than walking around an opera with a paper bag of pungent meat," she said with a sigh.

The waiter returned, and we sent back the aspic. She ordered lasagna, and I ordered pasta puttanesca.

"At least now I know what I'm getting into," she grumbled.

"Did you know that pasta puttanesca translates into 'pasta of the whore?'"

"You left nothing to the imagination on the first date, hon. Least of all your unveiled pasta references."

I nearly choked on my wine. I couldn't remember the last time I'd had such witty repartee with a date. Maybe since Morgan. Yes, I was certain of this now. That Juliet was not only the first person I'd opened myself up to in an intimate way after that ill-fated trip but also the first person I could have a good time with and feel challenged by. I craved the gravity of being completely relaxed in someone's presence paired with the pull of verbal sparring.

We talked on and on, nearly forgetting the time. I barely noticed when we started holding hands across the table or registered who had begun to run her nails along the other's palm. Yet I began to notice an odd straight couple sitting one table over, glaring angrily.

"I noticed them too. A long time ago," she said, noting the direction of my eyes.

"It's really starting to piss me off," I said. "They make it so obvious that they don't approve of us holding hands."

"Yeah, well, that's homophobes for you," she said, her voice lengthening with irritation.

We'd gone to great lengths to have a fairy-tale date, and now this pair's leering was sucking the fun out of everything. As if we should be ashamed.

The disapproving stares continued. Eventually, the bill arrived. I settled up and began to put my wallet back into my purse.

"Wait," Juliet said, catching my hand and lifting me out of my chair with chivalric grace. She leaned in and whispered, "I'll give them something to stare at."

Without warning, there in the middle of the restaurant, she pinned me against the wall and devoured me with her tongue—to the shock of the waiters who'd spent all night staring at her, the other patrons, and most of all, the odd Christian couple, who now looked as if they wanted to execute us in holy gay genocide. I could barely catch my breath; the world spun under her touch, and I was embarrassed, though not embarrassed enough to actually ask her to stop.

Just as suddenly as she'd initiated the intimacy, she grabbed me by the wrist and pulled me toward the door. We ran out of the restaurant and burst into giggles, fighting to breathe. She put her arm around my waist and pulled me close as we walked to the show. A fine drizzle misted raindrops into her hair.

Suddenly, I blurted out, "I don't mind if people stare as long as I'm with you."

She paused, a bit disarmed that I'd said that out loud. Then she gazed at me with wide and confused eyes. There was even a hint of fear in them. I can only play coy for so long. Then, like a child who isn't any good at playing the quiet game, I bubble over with excitement, say what I mean, and hope for the best. More often than not, it frightens the shit out of the other person. But I'd always figured that someone who would reject me for being forthright wasn't right for me in the first place.

"So what are we about to see?" she asked, changing the subject.

"Well, it's a series of opera and symphonic pieces in video games, written by a Japanese composer, Nobuo Uematsu."

"Ugh, video games. How could there be opera music in a video game?"

"You'd be surprised. Final Fantasy got an entire generation into the fine arts. Uematsu sometimes even has similarities to Mussorgsky."

Her eyes light up in delight.

"Oh, it's so nice to talk about music with someone who actually gets it. I'm more versed in classic rock, but this is interesting."

We took our seats near the stage. There was a seat empty next to her and two seats were empty next to me. A ponderously large gentleman eventually took the seat next to her.

Five minutes to showtime, the seats next to me remained empty.

But not for long. The same two homophobes who'd been glaring at us in the restaurant ended up taking those seats. Juliet and I looked at each other, wide-eyed and in shock, as the curtain began to rise.

Every now and then, I saw the couple stare over at us. Taking note, Juliet held my hand delicately and fully within their view, just as she had in the restaurant. She tossed her hair over her shoulder with a prideful smile.

We watched all of the pieces set to music. Her favorite was "Hymn of the Faith," the song for when a girl with the gift of magic must dance on sacred ocean waters and send the souls of a village's departed into the night sky. For once, I saw her shed that bored and jaded facade she liked to hide behind. She seemed excited, almost like a little child.

"Oh, I wish I had that power," she whispered in awe. "To dance and to touch a soul, send it to heaven."

My favorite came soon after: *Maria and Draco*. A mini opera about a prince from the west and a prince from the east who fight over a beautiful woman, Lady Maria.

She leaned over and whispered, "What are you thinking?"

"I'm thinking about how my whole life, since I first heard this mini opera, I wanted to be one of those princes and kiss the lovely Lady Maria."

"Hmm. Am I lovely to you? And a lady?"

She sat so close, her heat barely grazing against my skin, that I felt I was going to die.

"I will kiss you, then," she said, pulling me close by the necktie and cradling my face with her hand. I felt the stabs of hatred from the homophobes next to me. Meanwhile, the morbidly obese man sitting next to Juliet became wracked with sobs at the crescendo, his stomach flapping against her forearm.

"Ugh. What a sandwich." She sighed, pulling her lips from mine, and glared ahead at the stage.

I looked down and saw that her hand was still pressed in mine.

When we went home that night, I took off the tie and hung it on the horn of a ceramic ram I'd mounted against the wall. The accessory seemed to fit him. Juliet laughed and flung her panties over the other horn.

Everything seemed to be going well. We held each other all night. In the morning, we ordered in breakfast and sat together with coffee. She looked at me, then looked away, as if she were thinking about something.

"I guess this isn't a good time to say this. Maybe I should have said it sooner. But I'm seeing someone already."

Instantly, I felt a massive attack of lesbian PTSD. I fought to keep myself from dropping to the floor like a vet who'd served in 'Nam and was startled by the sound of a loud bang. *Great. It's happening again. Please, for the love of God, don't say you've had a husband for three years.*

"Uh . . . who is it? And how long have you been seeing them?" I said.

"I've been seeing a softball coach," she said. "But it's not what you think; she has a girlfriend and has been keeping me on the side for five years."

"So why don't you leave her?" I asked.

She got very serious.

"Look. I'm not leaving her for you."

"Uh, I didn't ask you to. I was just asking why, in five years, you wouldn't leave someone who keeps you as a mistress."

Her posture became defensive, and she looked at me with indignation.

"It's not like she's just 'keeping me as a mistress.' It's really complicated. I just thought you should know."

"Well . . . I would have preferred to know before we got involved," I said.

"I know. But now you know everything. It's getting late—I have to leave," she said. "Bye, babe."

She gave me a quick kiss, grabbed her coffee, and walked out the door. I went back to bed and stared at the tie hanging around the ram's horn. In my mind, it might as well have been a noose. I knew that a willingness to see someone on the side for five years indicated a deep love. A love that I could never compete with.

I met Juliet for lunch a few days later. She reached for my hand across the table.

Suddenly, I blurted out, "Don't you think it would be better if we were just friends?" She quickly withdrew.

"What are you saying?"

"I don't know. You've been seeing someone else for five years. Isn't it better this way?"

Her eyes welled with tears, and she looked around for an exit. The waiter came with the check. Juliet grabbed her purse and said, "Well, Esther, I think this one's on you." Then she stormed out the door.

I randomly tossed sixty dollars onto the clipboard and chased after her, then threw my arms around her.

"Come back. Don't do this." She fought back her tears and

moved her head away to hide the ones she'd already shed.

"There's nothing left to say," she said. "You said what you needed to, and so did I. I've got to get back to work."

She pushed me away and started walking down the sidewalk. I stood there watching her, unsure if I'd made the wrong or right decision. When she reached the end of the block, she turned, just to see if I was still there. I waved goodbye, but she just looked at me sadly and turned away.

Chapter
13

Star– Crossed Lovers

We broke it off like real lesbians: by inappropriately crossing blurred lines and doing lots of processing for an amount of time so significant that it annoyed anyone who would still listen. We didn't talk for a few weeks until she called and asked how I was doing. We started to chat about work, bad reality TV, pop culture. I thought maybe this could work. But then she sent me a sext, and having exactly zero willpower, I returned it. Sexts devolved into phone sex. Phone sex devolved into late-night hookups. But this time, the rules had changed: we were going to be Just Friends.

Like a reliable astrological prediction in any women's magazine, I can give you a rundown of how it continued. Being a Gemini, Juliet flitted about from lover to lover on a whim. Being an Aries, I wanted to be the best and tried to claim her as my own. She wanted to be friends with benefits, and I really didn't see the benefit in another friend. Our witty banter circled into mercurial jabs that started to hit lower and lower below the belt, even if we wouldn't get off the phone all night and stop texting each other all day.

Some nights, we couldn't stop chatting about the news, our brains flickering like little RSS feeds discussing current events. Most nights, we'd talk excitedly as soon as we got home from work about our favorite things or die laughing over trashy celebrity news. Other nights she'd call me drunk between the hours of one and three o'clock, ruminating about her dead father and his drinking. Or she'd call and serenade me with Lady Gaga songs on her guitar. And then there were the nights she'd call just to tell me about a girl on the subway with excellent tits she couldn't stop staring at, while I'd listen in silence and fury. After a pause, I'd retaliate and talk about someone I thought was equally fuckable. Then she would get quiet. Our conversations began to devolve in this way until Juliet called me one night at two o'clock, drunk again. I picked up the phone.

"Hello?"

"You're annoying," she slurred.

"Well, I was asleep, and that's a matter of taste, I guess."

"I just feel like you should know that. That sometimes, you are annoying to me. That's why we could never work out. Sometimes I think you'd be perfect girlfriend material, and at any other time in my life, I would be with just you. But then sometimes I think you annoy me. You can be so femme, so high maintenance. With your nail polish and glitter. Sometimes you flirt like a straight girl. I need a real dyke," she declared.

"I think the most annoying part of this conversation isn't that it's boring; it's that you woke me up. And PS: You have Viva La Juicy in your medicine cabinet. Maybe I'm the one who needs a real dyke," I said, hanging up the phone.

I remember waking up hours later and missing Morgan again, just when I'd thought I was making progress. For years Morgan and I had been no strangers to talking on the phone, and we never ran out of things to chat about. We had that level of compatibility. Yet, somehow, finding out Morgan hid an entire marriage to a man hurt less than being called annoying. Morgan never thought my nail polish or glitter were irritating. Often, we couldn't wait to tell each other about new eyeshadow palettes at Sephora that would increase the amount of glitter on our faces. I thought about the similarities between my two exes: both were well read, gorgeous, and funny in that quirky kind of way I adored. But Morgan was the only girl who'd loved me for me. She never asked me to be anything else. Then she just vanished.

Juliet and I tried for months to work things out. Sometimes when she threw another lover in my face, I had the audacity to submit a column to her about a date that I'd gone on. Our professional exchanges were different now on the phone. It used to take her thirty minutes to approve a column. Now it took four days. When I'd call to ask what needed to be fixed, she'd sigh. "Oh, you can do much better. There are just so many mistakes."

Now, she was the one to hang up.

Like any woman, I tried to process her feedback. I tried to reach for a deeper meaning, not getting that the writing was on the wall—and so were the track changes.

No one who was still reading my sporadically published column knew that the whole time I wrote about not wanting a stranger on some date, all I wanted was my editor. That whole time, my editor didn't want me or my writing.

There were so many mistakes. Every time we got close to each other, she'd pull away again. Sometimes I was the one who pulled away. Though I was a flirt, I was also more of a one-woman kind of woman. I might occasionally go on three dates in one weekend. But after realizing immediately who I did like and who I didn't, I would drop the others and choose just one. Juliet wasn't the same way. She held each of her lovers, bound and captivated, with her wit. Whenever I tried to escape (and I tried many times), I couldn't. Her smile and her charm wound their way into my heart; the more I flailed about in a panic, the more I failed at horribly incompatible dates where I couldn't get her out of my head.

She was notorious for her seduction. I once went on a morning jog and found her smoking on a stoop about three or four blocks from my apartment. She was seeing another girl who lived in my neighborhood. When I confronted her about it, she said she'd been seeing that girl for an entire year, before she met me. She'd only told me about the softball coach. Even then, I could not be released from her maddening attraction. There were nights when she went that girl's apartment, then called me up in the middle of the night, walked over to my apartment, fucked me, and went back to the other woman. Soon, there was another girl in the mix.

Over and over for months she regaled me with tales about the women she slept with as I kept my jealousy at bay. I tried to date around and couldn't. Eventually, I met a girl that looked like her doppelganger. That's when you really know you're not over someone.

Soon after, Juliet asked what I was up to. I said I was cleaning my apartment.

"So you're hooking up with someone else now," she said quietly.

"I didn't say that. I said someone is coming over tonight, and I'm mopping the floors."

"Is the girl single?" she asked.

"We've never slept together," I said.

"So this is a date. Or are you just hooking up with her tonight? Is that it?"

"We've never slept together," I repeated.

There was a pause.

"Please don't say any more. I don't need to know anything else," she said before hanging up.

The next morning at seven o'clock, she texted, "I have absorbed enough pain to last an entire lifetime."

After months of this, I was ready to try to forget her and decided to go out to Stonewall for a drink. The bar was empty except for one drag queen singing karaoke on a small stage.

I hadn't been there for more than fifteen minutes when Juliet walked into the bar on her first date with yet another woman. My heart fell into my stomach, and I tried to make a quick exit, but Juliet walked over and introduced us. I think her date could sense an uncomfortable pull between us. As it turned out, the woman on Juliet's arm was a senior editor for *Better Homes and Gardens* who shook my hand and immediately started bragging about her status and high pay.

"And what is it you do?" she asked.

I wanted to throw up. Sensing this, Juliet interjected and tried to save face.

"Esther is our renowned sex and dating columnist," she said, wearing that same contagious smirk as she emphasized *renowned*.

"Do you actually get paid for that? Is that a real job?" the other woman persisted incredulously. Juliet moved in to assist once more.

"Well, it's a small magazine; many of our writers aren't full-time staffers," she said in the familiarly soothing sex-operator voice.

"Don't worry; I, too, had to start at the bottom when I came to the city," the editor told me dismissively. "How long have you been doing this?"

"At least a year," I said, holding ground.

"Well, best of luck moving upward with your career," she said, looking at me as though I were a panhandler asking for spare change on the F train.

I glanced at Juliet, her contagious smirk beginning to catch.

I said, "Upward? Career? How could I ever ask for more?"

Juliet's eyes widened, and she turned her face slightly over a shoulder to hide her giggle. Her date glared at me in complete befuddlement.

"We'll be sitting over there if you'd like to join us for the evening," Juliet said, pointing to a table in a dark corner. I couldn't tell if she was being kind or humiliating me.

I said, "Sure, I'll be right there—I just need a drink" and went over to the bar. Phoebe was working. She was a reality-show contestant on NBC and a comedian in her off time. She was also a bit of a gossip and the first person to hear anybody's secrets at the bar. Talking to her, you'd learn anything you needed to know about a girl in seconds. I leaned into Phoebe's ear and whispered, "Please give me several glasses of whatever the strongest thing you have is. I honestly don't care what it is as long as it's the strongest thing in this entire bar."

She looked over my shoulder at Juliet's table.

"Oh my God. All these months, that's the girl you said you couldn't get over? If I had known, I would have warned you. Did you not know that she's the village bicycle? Even I nearly fucked her."

"Don't call her that," I hissed, trying to keep our voices down. "You know, she came over to my place one night, supposedly just for sex. But she ended up weaving a crown of honeysuckles into my hair and singing a song about my alleged beauty."

Phoebe threw up her hands and made a strangling motion at me. "I mean it. You need to get over her. She's bad news."

"Well, I'll never be over her, Phoebe. The sex was like 9/11. Never Forget."

Phoebe slammed down two shots.

"This is to ease the pain of being single," she said, shoving the first one toward me. "And this one is because you really, *really* fell for the wrong person this time."

I hurled the drinks down my throat.

"Look, I get it," I said. "But no matter what you say about her, I won't be able to think of Juliet as anything but the girl who put honeysuckles in my hair."

"Jesus. Get home safe, okay?"

I dashed out of the bar before Juliet and her date noticed I was gone, drunkenly cried on the streets of Greenwich Village, and ended up wasting eighty dollars on a psychic just to hear that I would die alone.

The next day, I logged onto OkCupid and attempted to get back on the market of the New York lesbian-dating scene. A daily email popped into my inbox. "We found five new matches for you!"

There, rated at 98 percent compatibility just for me, was the editor from *Better Homes and Gardens* who had resolutely kicked my ass the night before.

I hated that no matter how many times I tried to get away from Juliet, I couldn't ever quit her. Never before had someone generated such a chemical, almost primal attraction within me. Her eyes always drew me in, the way she'd smile as if we were two bad children up to no good. I stayed for her body language, the way she could look so alluring in a dress yet toss her hair and smoke Newports like a cocky man. Juliet was fully aware of her sex appeal, and she wielded it like a weapon. A weapon that was pointed at my heart.

Chapter
14

One Flew Over the Cuckold's Nest

Juliet went off on a vacation with the girl who lived two blocks away. I burned all over with hatred and decided that it was time to stop playing around. Straight girls say the best way to get over a man is to get under another one. I didn't see why the same couldn't be said about women.

I figured, why not out of the frying pan and into the fire? Enough with bars and apps, I'll stop being coy and going to a sex club, really and truly prove that I have no feelings and take back all of the power, this time. And yet, could I handle it? I had some experience hanging out in the leather scene in SF, yet some of the experiences that seemed like they were common for everyone else still somehow weren't for me. I'd get too shy, have an anxiety attack and flee for my life. For instance, every single lesbian in the world talked about having a threesome. Every. Single. One. I had a very *Are You There, God? It's Me*, Margaret moment and felt like the last girl in eighth grade waiting for her first period. The closest I ever got to a threesome was making out with two friends at the same time, which only happened because we were drunk. It ruined our friendships and happened nowhere near a leather bar. So I'm not really sure why I thought I could get laid at a sex club. These environments were always uncomfortable for me, and I probably would have had better luck picking up girls at the DMV or a dentist's office. And honestly, I didn't even want a threesome; innately, I'm too jealous to share a lover.

Still, my motto in life is that if it can't kill you, hurt another person, or land you in jail, it's worth trying once. Maybe a few times if you aren't really sure how you feel about it.

I started getting into BDSM in my early twenties after hanging with gay man friends at bars for leather daddies, like The Stud in the SoMa, which I liked to go to because they played awesome music. I remember an old man in a business suit who looked like Colonel Sanders would frequently come into The Stud and just shuffle by himself on the floor. His nickname around the bar was "the Senator" because we were convinced he was an uptight Republican from Arkansas with a secret fondness for butt plugs.

I liked to be dominated verbally or emotionally but not completely physically; that was one area where I liked to be in charge. I didn't like being slapped in the face. But I didn't really mind being called a whore. In general, I just liked aggression in bed, for hair to be pulled or for nails to scrape on skin, with lots of biting and begging. I wanted sex to feel like two pretty warriors struggling in the heat of battle. Yet, for all of the wrestling around, I still wanted soft kissing and for someone to run her hands through my hair.

Sometimes I liked to play a little harder, tie someone up and hold a dull blade to her throat while she was blindfolded.

And I didn't mind getting whipped. In fact, when I was younger and full of self-hatred, it was a way for me to externalize my pain, along with getting pierced. At my apex, I had fourteen piercings and two tattoos. Once, I went with a friend to a mixed dungeon party just for doms and subs. There, we approached a gorgeous dominatrix named Mistress Heart. She told me that it would cost money for her to beat me up. I thought, *Wow, this is great. Instead of buying a girl four hundred cosmos before finding out she isn't over her ex and is emotionally unavailable, I can pay a stranger to hurt me, and it's all been planned out from the very beginning.* A guy emerged and said he would pay both of us for the right to watch her beat me.

Angrily, I accepted. I hated when men wanted to watch me when I kissed girls on dates, and now this. I knew he was expecting her to barely tickle me with a feather or a tiny crop and for me to fall over helplessly so he could potentially masturbate to it later. I braced myself on the rack as she pulled out her flog.

Over and over, she cracked her whip at my bare back, and I didn't say my safe word. In my twenties, I was so numb with disgust for myself that the flog had no effect. I looked over. The guy's smile was beginning to fade. Mistress Heart pulled out a second flog and began to alternate between the two. Over and over, she lashed at me until I bled, and I still said nothing. Made no noise. Not even a whimper.

By this point, the guy's smile had completely disappeared; now he just looked horrified. He whispered to my friend, "She looks like she's really getting hurt. I don't think I want to watch this anymore. This has stopped being fun for me." Then he slipped my friend twenty dollars, I guess as some form of compensation. Only after he left did I raise my hand and ask the mistress to stop.

I just couldn't take it anymore. I couldn't take the pain of my frustration over being young and gay and alone.

So I decided it was time to kick things up a notch and try going to a party for women. In my wildest dreams, I would go to an S&M club and find a superhot gay girl who looked like Trinity from *The Matrix* wearing a full-body leather suit. I wanted nothing more than to put on a slave collar, be led around on a leash, and get yelled at or bossed around. To be told exactly how to please and serve a hot woman shouting insatiable, unrealistic demands. At thirty-seven, I now realize this is the oldest S&M game in history, and it's called marriage.

Reality was always distinctly different from fantasy. Whenever I went to kink events for women on the West Coast, everyone was dressed in business casual and sat around talking about their feelings like we were in therapy or AA. The last time I went to a lesbian sex party in San Francisco, everyone had to put a star on a name tag. The color of the star indicated what you were into or looking for. Your star might communicate that you were a dom or sub or looking for a one-night hookup, etc. As a joke, somebody said that the gold star meant, "Looking for the love of my life." I put it on my name tag because I was a gold star, and technically, I was always looking for the love of my life. Not only did I not get laid, I also fled the party with my friend after she saw her ex and panicked. We ended up buying a giant bag of chips at a bodega and talking about life on the street until two o'clock in the morning.

At least the girls on the East Coast dressed the part and looked really hot. I didn't know what to expect, walking into my first underground girl party in New York, I stepped inside a secretive basement-play space. The girls were all standing around in leather, watching TV. There was a snack table. I remember wondering why there was a buffet table at a sex club. Most of the snacks were high in sugar, so I think they were there to keep people from passing out after getting whipped or playing too hard. Only two girls were going at it, and they were clearly an exhibitionist couple.

A girl came up to me and said, "Just so you know, I think you're very cute."

I said, "Thanks! You are too."

Then we awkwardly stared at each other. She was a pretty brunette who was all tarted up and waiting in a tight corset.

But I couldn't consummate.

Why, after all these years, would I chicken out now? *Why can't I have some kind of emotional, intellectual connection with my anonymous sexual hookup?* I thought, bitterly. *It seems only two women in this world are allowed to cause immense pain and humiliate me semi consensually: Morgan and Juliet. Apparently, you can treat me like shit if you're funny. But I don't know if you can make me laugh—I don't know who you are. You're hot though. God.*

That was my tell, my open and obvious secret. That I was perhaps the world's sluttiest lesbian, but I was not really a slut—not in my heart. I was Julia Roberts in *Pretty Woman*! A hooker with a heart of gold. I didn't want next to nothing; I always wanted something more. Even when I casually hooked up with girls, I still sometimes wrote private poems and songs about them. But I never showed them what I wrote, I just threw everything away.

The pretty brunette was waiting for my next move. I just smiled politely and walked over to the snack table. There, I toppled a bowl of Twinkies, shoved the cakes into my purse quickly, like I was pulling off a bank heist, and ran out of the club as fast as possible with no explanation. I wanted adventure and a night of relentless, experimental passion where I wouldn't get my heart broken. Instead, I stole eleven snack cakes in public, then stayed up all night bundled up in a blanket while watching *X-Men: The Animated Series* (a '90s classic) with my cat. I was horny as hell, but I didn't want to get gangbanged in a warehouse by strangers. I wanted a familiar lover, one I could know intimately and be close with; I wanted Juliet by my side. I told myself that I would have to kill this longing. That maybe if I just kept fucking a bunch of people, I wouldn't miss her anymore.

Nothing filled the yearning.

When Juliet came back from her vacation, she texted and asked what I was doing.

Bitterly, I texted, "Oh, I'm fine. Just went to a sex club last night. That's all."

She drove over in the middle of the night and was in front of my apartment within half an hour to shout at me for my poor decision-making.

"Well, who fucking cares?" I screamed. "I didn't even hook up with anyone."

Juliet paused.

"You didn't?"

"No. I got scared. They had a snack table, like for a house party. So I stole all of the Twinkies, then went home and watched *X-Men*."

"They had Twinkies at a sex party?"

"They didn't after I left."

She blinked, then burst out laughing. I started to turn away and go back inside when she rushed at me and gave me a deep, soft kiss.

"Ooh. You taste like a Twinkie," she whispered.

"Maybe because I ate six of them," I said, pushing her away. "I hate you. I really do."

"Can I come upstairs and have one?" she asked, grinning sweetly. "I won't sleep with you, I promise."

"Ugh. You can have the other five," I said, letting her in.

Chapter
15

A Cry
for
Help

We hadn't talked in a few days. We'd gotten into our fifth (or eighth) loud argument, probably over yet another woman. Then we'd both spun off into gossipy benders who drank too much and asked our mutual friends what the other was doing (yet never bothered to break the stalemate and call each other.)

This seventy-two hour impasse included not exchanging any posts on Facebook. To anyone under thirty in 2012, this was the equivalent of a decade of silence. I wondered what Juliet was up to. *Probably prowling the Village with another girl*, I thought. Maybe even that awful *Better Homes and Gardens* editor. I wondered if she missed me, or if she was just banging this preposterous woman from Massachusetts who thought the virtue of hailing from Nantucket was akin to being a British rock star with long hair in 1969.

I tried to go on more dates that didn't shake me. There was the graphic designer, the English teacher, the real estate agent, the six-foot-tall amazon: another goddamned Gemini who loved anime but gave me a terrible and ill-timed back massage to "Born this Way." Her body was so lengthy to wander that I felt a need to cry out in the darkness for Siri to please give me directions to her pussy because I'd been kissing her thighs for what felt like half an hour, and I already had lockjaw.

I failed to move on. But Juliet always seemed so happy with the others.

Suddenly, I got a text. "Can you please call me? I need to talk to you."

I paused. It wasn't like her to be so direct and urgent. So I picked up the phone.

"What's up?"

She started laughing casually. "I tried to kill myself three days ago. Haha."

I wondered why she was laughing. Was this a joke?

"Come on," I said. The laughter died down.

"No, I did, I just . . . I don't know. I can't deal with the general pressures of being alive, I guess. I thought it would be better if I went off to be with my grandmother. Or my dad. So I took a bottle full of Klonopin and passed out on the floor. I woke up this morning and spent the whole day vomiting in the bathroom."

My heart caught in my throat.

"Are you crazy? Why would you do something like that?" I screamed. "Did you go to the hospital?"

"Uh, no, actually the first thing I did was go for a run. Along the way, I came across a church. I thought about going inside, talking to someone. I nearly died, Esther. Maybe I should just give my life to God." She started laughing again, but her laugh frightened me. So delicate and unsettling, like a desiccated butterfly using its last electrical impulses to move its wings again.

"Maybe you should talk to somebody," I said.

"What, like go inside and talk to the priest? I thought about it. But I was all sweaty from my run, and I wasn't wearing a sports bra. It's already bad enough that I'm gay; I don't need to be even more disrespectful to God. I'm a Catholic-Italian girl. Like Madonna."

I tried to hold back, but I started crying.

"Don't ever do that again," I sobbed.

"Look, I'm fine!" she shouted. Like it was all normal and I was nagging her for not taking out the garbage. "I'm getting in the shower."

"All right. Bye," I said. Not knowing what else to do, I called the Chief. She was our den mother, the lesbian equivalent of Big Mama in Chicago. The Chief was older and wiser; she knew how to handle everything. Surely she'd know how to deal with lesbian drama.

"Go to her," the Chief said. "Don't let her be alone right now. I'm going to organize some kind of intervention. You're not the only one that's been noticing this getting out of control. You did the right thing in telling me, Esther. Do you know what this is? It's a cry for help. You can't do this alone. We'll take care of it together. But go uptown right now, while I figure this whole thing out."

Ironically, I'd been running on a treadmill when Juliet texted. Both of us viewed our own bodies and faces with such scrutiny—yet thrived off the worship the other generated sexually. There must have been some beauty within each of us to spark this attraction. Yet neither of us could see her own. I rushed to the gym shower, quickly got dressed, and went uptown with damp hair. On the way, I briefly worried about her seeing me look so disheveled. *If she sees me like this, she won't like me anymore*, I thought. Then I realized her life was at stake and my appearance probably didn't matter.

When I stepped out of the elevator, I went quickly down the hall to Juliet's apartment and knocked on the door. No answer. I heard movement behind the door, then footsteps walking away.

"Juliet, please. Open this door," I said. "Please."

I waited for twenty minutes, knocking and then finally banging. "Fine!" she shouted.

When she opened the door, I saw that the apartment was completely dark and looked as if it hadn't been cleaned in a while. Her numerous books were all over the place. The room stank of beer and vomit.

She lay down on the floor and began to rub her temples in silence.

"Hey, let's get out of here," I said quietly. "Let's get out of this apartment. There's a good place nearby that I always wanted to try. Will you have dinner with me?"

She said nothing and kept rubbing her head. I didn't know what else to say, so I sat next to her in the dark. There was another thirty minutes of silence. She continued laying there and acting as if I didn't exist. Her cat crawled out from under her bed. He seemed distressed, meowing loudly and walking between the two of us, as if he were pleading with me to help her.

"Juliet, please. I think we need to take you to a doctor. Or a fine restaurant. I don't know. Just please, come on. For me."

Suddenly her eyelids snapped open, and all I could see in the dark were the whites of her eyes, the ferocity and terror radiating through the same blue that had captivated me. Her gaze was sharp and cold, like an edge of black ice down a long, dark road.

"*Get out!*" she screamed at the top of her lungs as she flew at me. Startled, I got to my feet and backed away quickly. "Get out. Get out. *Get out!*"

I didn't say anything. She pushed me hard out of her front door, and I heard the bolt on the other side click. Not knowing what else to do, I went to the restaurant. When the waitress came over, I panicked and ordered cornbread and banana pudding. She gave me an odd look. After a while I couldn't compose myself in public anymore and just cried, my tears spilling onto the plate.

That evening, I called the Chief and told her what had happened. She gathered a small cadre of Juliet's friends who were all ready to convey their worries to her during a meeting later in the week. I wasn't invited, and I understood why, but it felt wrong. The Chief said I'd already expressed what I needed to that night when I went to her apartment.

A few days later, I didn't get a text. I got a call.

"You did this to me!" Juliet shrieked. "Turned everyone against me!"

"I didn't," I stammered. "I was worried about you. I care for you—"

"Well, it got me fired from *GRL*. Are you happy? This is all your fault! I never want to see you again! I hate you. *You are sick! You are mentally ill*," she roared.

"What did you expect me to do?" I shouted back. "I was trying to help. You told me you wanted to kill yourself! What was I supposed to do with that information? Just shrug and chuckle about you not going into a church because your boobs were sweaty? You don't want to see me anymore, fine. I get it. Don't worry. I'll stay far away from now on."

Chapter
16

Eat It Like You're in Jersey

Two months had passed, and I'd started living in a quiet hermitage like a monk. Slowly, I tried to focus on habits that felt healthier. Less drinking, more trips to the gym. Getting a therapist and wasting vast swaths of her life complaining about my issues. Going back to reading the classics.

I was preparing for another thrilling evening of being single and playing video games when Juliet randomly called and asked if I wanted to go for a drink at Stonewall. I hadn't heard a word from her since our last phone call.

After talking about it, I agreed to meet her. I couldn't help it; I wanted to see her. I missed her terribly.

She texted me for three hours, begging for me to come out.

"Come out and dance with me tonight. We'll just be friends," she said, ever so playfully. "And please do come with your eyeliner dark and smoky. I love when my friends do that."

"We can't do this again," I said.

"If you come out and meet me, I'll dress like a Jersey girl from the '80s," she said.

"Oh, fine," I said, giving in.

It was raining in the city, and Juliet had naturally curly hair that she straightened every day—but when it rained, to no avail. Sure enough, when I met her outside, she teased her bouncy hair, wearing skinny jeans with boots and a biker jacket.

"You wore your eyeliner smoky. Well, I held up my end of the deal," she said, making a grand, sweeping gesture at her outfit. If a girl was femme and aggressive, read good books, or was from New Jersey, that was usually all it took for me to board the express NJ TRANSIT train to Fucksville.

Since she'd lost her job at the magazine, Juliet had started working at a barbecue restaurant as a waitress. I felt a deep sadness when she told me this. There were times that she'd go out for a "martini lunch" when we dated and not come back for two hours. I'd heard stories that she wasn't showing up to work or answering her phone. During the long periods after another fight, I constantly got calls asking if I knew where she was, and I never did.

She'd lost a lot of weight. I looked at how thin she'd become and tried to guess just how much. Maybe she saw me staring. Out of nowhere, she said she'd lost about thirty pounds.

"I measured my distance at work, and on average I walk twenty-eight freaking miles to serve people ribs every night," she said with a sigh.

There was a new piercing since the last time we'd talked. A Monroe. And two new tattoos. One was a guitar pick on her right wrist, in memory of her dead father. The other was the sign of Gemini on the opposite wrist.

"It's on my left wrist because in Italian superstition, the left hand is evil. *La sinistra*. So it's there to remind me of duality. If

I've been bad, it's not too late to do some good. And if I've been particularly good, it's okay to be a little bad." She winked.

Then she turned my head and looked at my ear.

"You've gotten rid of some of yours."

I didn't tell her that every time we didn't speak, I did the opposite of what I'd done in the past. When I started to feel happier, I removed a piercing rather than wounding myself with a new one to feel something. The goal was to slowly get rid of them all until at least the visible ones were gone. Then, somehow, to be clean again.

"Well, I didn't get rid of the ones that matter." I smirked.

When Juliet wanted to go out for another smoke, she took her jacket off and put it on me. Which was ridiculous because I was wearing warmer clothing then, as she put it, "her Jersey cleavage shirt," which bared like three-fourths of her massive breasts. She was shivering to death. I took the jacket off and put it back on her, but she just flung it over my head and laughed.

"Fine. Then I'll stand close to you to warm you," I said.

She and her large hair puffed on Newports as per every Jersey stereotype in the book. She grinned. "That's better. I like the heat you're getting off. Aargh. I mean giving off."

At the exact same time and in the same tone of voice, we said, "Freudian slip."

"*Damn it.* We aren't even girlfriends; it's not like we can do the lesbian merge thing," she said.

We decided to walk around the block and catch up. I noticed a U-Haul truck parked on the curb.

"Oh my God," she said. "Please take a picture with me in front of the U-Haul, and I'll pretend to be your girlfriend. It's funny because it'll never happen."

We posed and laughed because the photo turned out looking unbelievable and like total shit. I couldn't tell if she was flirting or just reminding me for the thousandth time that we were the worst match ever. Even OkCupid said so. Whenever I searched, she always popped up in the same whopping 100 results.

When I clicked on her profile, the algorithm rated us as 90 percent friends, 90 percent enemies, and 60 percent compatibility as lovers.

We went back inside the bar. After having a few drinks, I couldn't stand just looking at her, so I sat close and put my head on her shoulder.

She leaned in and gave me one of those sweet, soft kisses that felt as though it would strike me dead. Another electric volt.

We ended up kissing for at least an hour in a dark corner.

"I love the way you kiss," she whispered. "I haven't felt one like that in so many years."

It hit me that exactly one year ago we'd met for the first time at Stonewall, and right after our first kiss, she'd said those same words. Was she telling me the truth, or was this just a line she said to all the girls?

Still, the words gnawed at my heart because every time we kissed, I thought the same thing. That I loved it and could kiss and kiss her for whole hours; that nobody had made me feel this way in so long. I couldn't name the last time I'd had a kiss that leveled me. Maybe, conversely to so many things back then, it was a first.

Of course, we ended up going back to her place. She heated up a plate of White Castle hamburgers and set them before me.

"Eat it like you're in Jersey," she said.

That was all I needed to hear. We fucked all night again. I'd thought we were through with this, yet I still didn't want to be.

When I woke up the next morning, it was to the sound of raging, howling winds at her window. There was a storm advisory throughout New York. I was shivering, and she pulled me close by the waist and held me tight. "You were so far. Come cuddle me; I'll keep you warm," she said.

This was different. The last time we'd hooked up, we'd had a kind of hate sex, so we slept on opposite sides of the bed with our backs turned to each other.

But all throughout the previous night, she had reached for me and pulled me into her arms. The whole night, she'd never let me go. And she'd never done that before.

Eventually, she started getting texts on her phone because she was supposed to meet a friend for brunch. She canceled to stay in with me. I felt bad because her friend was upset about it, and I knew firsthand how annoying Juliet's flakiness could be. But I was also secretly happy that she was making time for me.

Still, I was afraid she'd soon tell me to go since we didn't usually linger long. So, after a couple of hours, I put on my clothes and got ready to leave. I didn't want to suffer rejection and admit defeat to her again.

"Wait," she said as I was putting on my pants. "Don't go. I was wondering if maybe you wanted to watch a movie with me and cuddle more."

I smiled, relieved.

"Pick a DVD from over there," she said.

I came back with a case and tossed it on the bed. *Grumpier Old Men.*

"*Marry me right now.* We're getting married!" she said, pulling me back in and covering me with kisses.

We watched maybe the first fifteen minutes of it until we ended up fucking again, limbs intertwined with so many whispers and touches.

The way we had sex this time was different from when we would usually get raunchy and come. This time she couldn't stop holding me after one of us finished and kissing me everywhere, smoothing my hair. More tender than when we'd call each other worthless nobodies. This time, neither of us uttered an insult. I liked it, but I also didn't understand it. Something felt like it had shifted between us; I couldn't let down my guard.

Eventually, I did have to go, and she had a work shift. We kissed goodbye all the way to the door.

Before I left I looked out her window at New York City and thought about how Juliet and I would never be girlfriends. I knew we didn't have a future together. We'd hurt each other deeply, back and forth in our warlike fights, and we'd thrown umpteen amounts of women in each other's faces like grenades of dismissal. This time, something in her touch and embrace had drawn me in deeper and shown more of her vulnerability than any time before, yet I felt something else fading and falling apart. I can't explain it, but there's always that moment when you hook up with somebody for the last time and know in your soul that it won't ever happen again. That it really is the last time. The end. Even if you don't want it to be. This was that time.

I thought then that at some point in the future, I would look back and think of me and Juliet in our late twenties, two girls living alone in the world's biggest city who occasionally kept each other warm.

Chapter
17

Caught in a Bad Romance

A week later, I was sitting in a sports bar called Canz, a place that was essentially the warmed-down, low-budget version of Hooters, with Leah, my totally heterosexual, platonic wife. We had nothing better to do than order a gigantic blue fishbowl cocktail and people watch the gross men who unironically frequented this establishment.

My phone buzzed with a text from Juliet. She casually mentioned that she had gone back to Jersey for the weekend on a mini vacation to visit her mom. We went through the motions of asking each other how our days had gone.

Then, without warning, she texted, "I do love you, you know. Thank you for looking out for me."

I took a deep breath, pondering this turn of events. After an entire year of repeatedly being told she'd never want to be more than friends with benefits, was this a concrete admission of her real and true feelings?

"Love you too," I texted back awkwardly. It didn't quite feel like the right thing to say, yet I was relieved to type it.

"I really do. I mean it. Thank you for always being there for me."

I thought of a quote by Rilke. *That's love: Two lonely persons keep each other safe and touch each other and talk to each other.*"

"We need to keep each other safe," I wrote. I didn't tell her that I'd gotten the line from Rilke.

After finishing our gigantic aquarium of booze, Leah and I gave each other hugs, and I started a long moonlight walk back home. I wondered if I'd said the right thing to Juliet. Although I spent every day and night thinking—and, often, worrying—about her, did I truly feel love? Perhaps it was love, but simply an unhealthy one. Never before had I felt such a strong affection that I couldn't properly name. Could the very definition of love be as simple as Rilke had said?

I wasn't sure. I knew the pain I felt was more than like but less than love for someone who didn't know or care about how much I ached all over. I burned with anger, thinking, *I don't want to do this. I don't want to love you. I don't want to love you. I'm pleading with heaven and earth every single day just to not like you.*

When I got home, I sat out on the fire escape and looked at the moon. Where could Juliet and I even go from here? I wasn't sure if our exchange was merely another in a drunken string of soon-to-be-forgotten declarations. If she had meant what she'd said, could we try to be together? Could I ever trust her?

Juliet called the next day complaining of a major hangover, just as I was nursing my own. I'd stayed up all night drinking whipped cream vodka and writing my second draft of a trashy romance novel that I never had the courage to submit to a publisher, thinking that perhaps if I could meditate on how these characters loved one another, I'd understand my own feelings better.

I asked Juliet how much she'd had to drink.

She admitted she'd had quite a bit—before subsequently getting into a threesome with her best friend and a new woman who seemed to have come out of nowhere.

I was gutted.

"Do you even remember what you said to me last night?"

She seemed legitimately confused. "What are you talking about?"

"You told me that you loved me," I said. My stomach lurched, and I was reminded of other times she'd called me up in the middle of the night to drunkenly sob about how, if we had met at any other time in life, I would have made the perfect girlfriend. She claimed she would have snatched me up in an instant. The next morning, she always denied she'd said these things.

"Oh, that. I meant I love you as a person. You're a beautiful person. I'll never be able to love you in *that* way. You know that, right?"

A person? She loved me like she could love any ordinary human being on the street, just for existing? How was it that my previous editor, a fine purveyor of literature who'd worked in the actual business of words, had selected the worst possible word to utter?

I'd been willing to overlook so much. The drugs. The times she called me a "kinky Oriental" when she was drunk and slurring. *Just a joke.* The other girls. The suicide attempts. Her subpar outcry for her entire life's existential depression, the grave tragedy of being white, blonde, and pretty yet needing more medication to erase the glamorous ennui of her own trendy fragility. The pills, and the pills, and the pills.

I'd done it because I thought, somewhere deep inside, there was a small amount of love between us. Not everything was casual; something had to be right. Two femme writers, gay, with an almost religious zeal for words and knowledge, beauty and art, comedy and drama. We were the glittering third rail current running through New York City at night and between each other. It was all meant to be, until it wasn't. How could she, my lover and my friend? *A person.* My rival. *In all of your enviable skill, how could you possibly have chosen the worst word of all?*

But I wasn't special to her; I was only another notch on her bedpost, a forgettable pop song that had briefly sored to the top of the charts but soon would be forgotten. In no alternate dimension would there ever be a day when one of us would have to remember to pick up cat food and TP on the way home. We'd screwed each other over—literally and metaphorically—enough times to make sure that never happened. I just didn't want to let go, didn't know how to.

In that moment, I thought it didn't matter if I died—there was nothing left within me anymore. Nothing to offer someone else, nothing to offer myself. What had she believed would come out of this situation? Did she think after a year of hooking up we would just laugh it off, get our nails done at the Jersey Shore, and share puns over Bloody Marys? Could she not see that I'd let her peek into my soul, that it wasn't just sex, that I hadn't let anyone so close in at least three years? In my mind, we couldn't go from late-night marathon sex and two o'clock in the morning phone confessionals to pretending none of it had ever happened.

But maybe she could. Just like New York itself could. People swapped and dropped lovers all the time. Why couldn't I do that too? Perhaps it was normal to talk to someone on the phone almost every day until the wee hours, fuck their brains out for nearly a year, and then tell them that, obviously, it was all platonic. Perhaps I was insane.

I wanted to tell her, "I wish we had never met. Why did you come into my life and make me feel anything just to be like everyone else who has ever done this to me? You were supposed to be different. I believed in you."

Instead, I just screamed at the top of my lungs, "I hate you! Don't call me up at one o'clock crying about being alone anymore. You're not lonely. You haven't even spent one minute in what it truly feels like to be alone. There are so many people coming in and out of your bed that you're like a prostitute. You say I have self-esteem issues because I can't stand all of this. Well, maybe you have the self-esteem issues. Exactly how many people do you need to sleep with to feel good about yourself?"

"Oh, stop it," she said with a nonchalant acidity I hated. "You're so self-pitying. All you ever do is cry about how you're alone and you're always going to be alone. What, do you think you're this shining knight and everyone else around you is a horrible bitch who just does terrible things to you and laughs maniacally afterward?"

"Name one fucking thing I have done to you," I said. "Go on! Name it! You're no different than anyone else I've had feelings for. No different. If I'm so horrible, then stop coming back to me; just leave me alone. Stop intentionally hurting me. Just leave me alone!"

This time, she remained silent.

"And don't tell me I'm self-pitying," I shouted. "I don't have a mom to run to who coddles me and posts pictures of us on Facebook. I basically have fucking nothing. There really is no one who loves me, who even checks on me. Months go by where I could be dead and no one would even know. And I don't have to use pills or people as crutches. I take the fucking pain, and I'm stronger than you'll ever be. You're just a weak person. And you will never, ever stand on your own."

There was a long pause on the other side of the line.

"You've just said some of the meanest things I've ever heard anyone say to me," she said. "Does it make you feel better to call me weak? I know that I'm a weak person. You don't have to tell me something I've known for my whole life. So many people in my bed that I'm like a prostitute? Saying you're stronger than I'll ever be? You don't have to say it. And you *do* mean something to me. If you didn't, I wouldn't keep coming back like this. Even after the first or second time you went away. I miss you when we don't talk, and I keep coming back because we have a lot of common interests and the same sense of humor. I like having you in my life."

I'd gone too far. Yet I knew I couldn't have restrained the words if I'd tried.

Because I was never crueler to Juliet than I was to myself.

"Maybe I can't be in your life until I'm with someone who loves me," I said. "Because I'm happier without you."

"Everyone is worn down. It's cute that you're trying to open yourself up and be close to people, but most women are even more emotionally unavailable than I am," Juliet said.

I heard the click of her lighting another Newport and the whoosh of her blowing out a long puff of smoke.

"Someday I might find someone who loves me, even if you don't. Maybe even someone who loves me as more than just a person," I said.

There wasn't a sound between us except the sizzle of her cigarette as she took another drag.

"The loss is mine, I'm sure."

I never tell anyone who's hurt me when I've finally decided to walk away. That's because I know it hurts more when they reach out and hear nothing, forever.

"Will you text me tomorrow? I'll text you," she said, as though we hadn't just destroyed each other in a veritable lesbian World War III.

That was the last night I ever spoke to her. I never saw Juliet again. About two months later, the Chief mysteriously requested my presence at her apartment in the middle of the night. We talked about how Juliet was starting to become a drug addict, how she was going downhill, and how to get her help. I didn't tell the Chief that losing Juliet and really grasping what we'd done to each other over a year had made me want to die. The Chief started to google rehabs that looked like palaces. She let it slip that Juliet was sleeping with even more people than she'd been with before and now had two girlfriends on top of extra lovers.

"Lovely," I said, rolling my eyes.

"Think of someone other than yourself," the Chief shouted. "She needs our help! Stop being so selfish!"

I burst into tears. "What do you want me to say? Maybe I need to be selfish! I spent a year thinking only of her, answering the phone at three o'clock in the morning when she called drunk or high, and now I'm forgetting who I am. Do you even know how many nights I went out to the Village trying to pick up someone else and forget about her? Well, I'm thirty, and it's too late now. I'm just going to die alone," I screamed.

"No, you'll find someone. You will," the Chief said, holding me as I sobbed. "She had real feelings for you, you know."

"Bullshit," I said. "You don't have to make up things to make me feel better."

"I'm not making anything up. She said she was starting to love you and that it scared her. If she would have turned her life around for anyone, it would have been you."

I stopped crying, folded my arms, and looked out the window.

"We had a serious talk about you," the Chief said.

"Oh?" I asked, snapping up the bait. "What did she say?"

"She said she felt terrible for what she did, that she realized she destroyed you. I told her, 'Esther's not a victim. She's seeing new people, and she's moving on.'"

"What did she say to that?" I asked.

"Nothing. She just cried," the Chief said.

I didn't know whether or not to believe the Chief, if it was all some sweet little improv fiction she'd spun to get me to stop crying. The Chief couldn't stand to see a woman's tears.

I later told the Chief that I wished her well but could no longer be a part of the magazine. It really was my time to move on. I knew I couldn't do that without severing every possible connection to Juliet.

Years later, Juliet started a public blog and wrote about how, at that time in her life, she got addicted to opiates and tried to kill herself three times. When I read that blog, I felt a deep guilt and shame that maybe I'd contributed to her problem.

But I'd loved her, I'd listened to her problems for an entire year, and I hadn't known what else to do with my unrequited love but be chaotic and insane. And the Chief's story rang true in only one verifiable sense: Juliet did destroy me. I was no longer the shy girl who'd come to New York on a wing and a prayer, afraid to get somebody's number at the bar. A year and a half had passed since I started the blog, and in the months after the final blowout, I lost control. Now I sometimes had three or four dates on the weekend; all I did was fuck girls and tell them I never wanted anything more from them. In the same way Juliet once used her tender seduction as a weapon pointed at my heart, I began to generate a gravity of lust that pulled any heavenly bodies toward me and crushed them with cold, centrifugal force.

On the train, I thought of that last night when we met up at Stonewall, danced to Lady Gaga's "Bad Romance," and took turns lip syncing about how we didn't want to be friends into an invisible microphone.

Afterward we fell backward onto a couch, laughing hysterically at being dysfunctional lesbians and then wildly making out two minutes later. We wrote that bad romance. We revised it over and over and over again in fits of jealous red pen, trying to come up with a final draft, then ended up tossing it into a dumpster fire of lesbian drama. I wonder sometimes if it could have ever ended up any other way.

In the end, what woman can do anything constructive or mature with a love that will never be returned? We're all insane. Sappho once said, "The dice of love are shouting and madness." That's how you know Sappho probably fucked every student at her academy. She probably just fucked them all.

Chapter
18

I ‹3
NY

I returned to old habits and eviscerated myself. There's a tattoo that wraps around my ankle. It says, "Seduce and Destroy." It was meant, in my twenty-four-year-old wisdom, to look edgy and foreboding, frightening off anybody who thought it might be easy to manipulate me and break my heart. But I secretly intended a double, inverse meaning: seduce and destroy myself. Inside I despaired, nursing my shame at a straight bar so no other lesbian in the city would gossip about how badly I'd fallen apart.

On one night a man with an open shirt and an oddly waxed chest asked if he could buy me a drink. I nearly left until I overheard a straight girl mutter, "Why is he into *her*, she's ugly and weird."

Then I vowed to give him tongue just to annoy her. I hadn't kissed a man in over a decade, and it felt like the last thing I could do to throw away my hopes and dreams of ever being able to live happily ever after with another woman. *Kissing a guy is like suicide*, I thought. *I'll jump.*

He leaned over and kissed me. I reached down—no boobs. Kissing a man when you're gay is like drinking a Diet Coke left out in the sun for five hours.

I disconnected from my body. In that moment, it felt like I was having a near-death experience. I thought about flashes of good times and bad times in a little montage, about all of the times people told me there was nothing left worth fighting for. About my ex who told me I would never find love. About some girl in a bar who gave up dating women because she wanted to have babies, then told me I was being "a stupid child" by believing I'd find a nice gay and get married.

In the vastness of this dissociation, I thought of just one girl: Morgan. The great love of my life, the One Who Got Away. The one whose love lost drove me to move across the entire country.

In retrospect, our dalliance was hilarious in that it was deeply sad. The best way I can describe two Aries femmes in heat is that we were like two sentimental children with Tourette's: we repeatedly got overwhelmed with excitement and felt a need to blurt out the extent of our true feelings for each other in random, inappropriate outbursts, then run screaming in another direction out of fear of what the other would say.

No woman prepared me for Morgan; her love was terror. Never before had such an intoxicating beauty and seamless intellectual/emotional compatibility captivated me so. To look upon her was not simply to be inspired but to be lost in the vast wilds of her grace. To love her was to fear mortality and know my own end.

I daydreamed about that last trip I took to Chicago, when I'd been ready to tell her the truth and put my feelings on the line. We were walking to an art museum when she rushed up behind me, threw her arms around my waist, and said, "I'm so happy; I can't believe you're actually here!" She did a breathless little giggle into my ear.

I wanted to turn around and throw her against the wall with kisses, or maybe awkwardly yell out, "Um, uh, I'm in love with you!"

But I didn't do anything. I stayed there in her arms, and I'd never felt so safe in my entire life. I stayed there and let the chance pass.

That's the moment I went back to when the man at the bar kissed me. I condensed it, froze it in time, and mentally created a divergent reality wherein I turned around and kissed her. In that timeline, I never got my heart broken, but I also never moved to New York. In that timeline, I moved to Chicago, killed elk with my bare teeth, and rolled around in animal pelts to keep warm in the winter, like a real Midwestern lesbian.

That divergent reality soared into the stars—and it touched another star, and another star, and another star—until it created a constellation of pointillism and light where our lips touched and our fingers interlocked in the night sky. I thought, *Let me stay here forever with you. I don't want to go back. Let it be just you and me this time.*

Something wrapped around my ankles—it was gravitational inertia ripping me from her heavenly body. Our lips parted, my hand slipped from hers, and I started to freefall through the inky depths, hurtling past the clouds and soaring through the sky. I could not stop the fall; there was nothing to grasp until reality cracked my skull wide open. Reality was a strange man in a dark bar, and his tongue was in my mouth.

I felt something wet pooling on my cheeks. It took a moment for me to realize tears were forming.

I slightly turned my head and wiped them on my sleeve, afraid of offending him of all things. Then I gently pushed his waxed chest, and only one word tumbled out of my mouth:

"No."

I got up and began to stagger out of the bar.

He chased after me and stood in the threshold as I walked down the street. The wind carried his open white shirt so that it looked like the billowing sails of a corsair's ship, even further cementing the image of him on the cover of a Danielle Steel novel or a '90s R & B video.

"Where are you going?" he called out.

"I've gotta get out of here," I mumbled cryptically. "To somewhere. Anywhere."

I gave up all hope after that night. I never went to another lesbian bar, ever again. I'd been dubbed one of *Time Out*'s "Most Eligible Lesbian Bachelorettes" and was *still* single at thirty, in an era where gay marriage was now legal, so I was truly fucked.

And I still hadn't caused myself enough injury. Another night at three o'clock I went to the aptly named Addiction NYC on St. Marks Place and got my nipples pierced a second time. When I woke up, there was blood on the sheets, blood all over the shower, blood everywhere. Yet I craved more; I still hadn't paid for the sin of being loved as *a person* with enough violence. I didn't want to ask for help, just couldn't—so I slowly stopped returning everybody's calls and turned off my phone for days at a time, retreating into the ritual of writing.

Days and nights, weeks and months passed, and I stayed shut in my apartment writing romance novels, sometimes staying up all night drinking a cocktail I invented called "The Secaucus Tease" in honor of the Jersey Girls (mix one part whipped cream–flavored vodka with one part cherry soda, and it's a party in your mouth. Just like a girl from Hoboken). I couldn't stop writing about love because not writing about it anymore meant accepting that I would die without it.

On those nights I'd occasionally take a break from writing, sit on the fire escape, and stare off into the sky, wishing on the few stars that pierced through the light pollution.

I kept going and going every night until four o'clock, sometimes beyond and into the wee hours. I couldn't control myself anymore. I soon realized that I wasn't tapping at my keys; I was banging on them and broke the T off my keyboard. How strange to be writing dozens of pages of romance in a rage, almost like bloodlust.

There was a tiny voice inside me, one that sounded suspiciously like my dad. The voice said, "You are stupid, you are ugly, and you are a failure. Did you really think you would come to New York and be a writer? Do you really think a series of romance novels will mean something to anyone, require any skill to write? Did you think someone like Juliet would ever *love* you?"

When I wrote, it felt as if a freight train was crashing into my brain, and the more I roared forth about breathless sighs and heaving bosoms, the tinier and more insignificant the voice became. It got smaller and smaller until I told the voice, "You aren't real. My passions are real. A stack of nine hundred pages sitting in a binder is real. This love will be allowed to live, even if it's just inside my head. You're nothing but an impotent voice, and you are the voice of someone who's dead. It doesn't matter if she doesn't love me. I'll continue this relentless onslaught. And even if I die alone, even if no one ever loves me, I will learn to love myself."

Little by little, I started to take myself on the dates that I secretly wished someone would take me on. Jell-O shots and *Spider-Man* on Broadway? Well don't threaten *me* with a good time. On a random Friday night, I put on makeup, did my nails, donned a glittery snakeskin top, and went to see the worst possible show ever—just because it was fun and I knew there couldn't possibly be a woman alive who would do something so stupid with me. Afterward, I walked over to a long line of pedicabs and chose the only one with leopard-print upholstery. The cabbie asked where I wanted to go, and I asked him to take me all the way up to Fifty-Seventh Street.

Panting like a gallop unchained, he ferried me up the street, a million LCD screens lighting the path. A bachelorette party in a pink SUV honked as they waved their penis lollipops out the window. I blew them a kiss, said congratulations on getting hitched, and told the guy I'd tip him extra if he ran faster so we could get away from them.

In that instant, my heartbeat quickened, and I actually blushed. The classic glamour of New York made me feel like I had a chance at making out with a totally overdone showgirl with a bad reputation. One who loved millions of people but maybe right now was just loving me. *As a person.*

The cabbie broke free from the bachelorette's entourage, but I took a minute to look around and feel the pulse of the city. Stimulation overload. *Is this what love is?*

Maybe love is buying a single ticket to watch *Spider-Man* on Broadway on a Friday night and taking a leopard-print pedicab as a personal chariot under all of Times Square's strobing advertisements. Maybe it's getting the most ostentatious, glittery nail polish at the salon and reading terrible 1950s lesbian romance on the couch during a thunderstorm. Maybe its quitting a temp job where I'm not valued. Or flirting with strangers, not taking things too seriously, and running away on my own terms afterward. Maybe it's grabbing an egg-and-cheese bagel at a bodega, then blasting EDM during the walk of shame at seven thirty in the morning.

But I know it's not. Because it's really the friends I made while working hard on my writing in the city, the supposedly crotchety New Yorkers who never once let me down. Catalina getting two tickets to a comedy show to cheer me up and listening to me blather on for an hour at dinner about how Judy Gold secretly has the most sex appeal in the entire universe. The Chief and her zany, madcap, three o'clock in the morning plans that somehow always worked. Chris, the Silver Fox, with her tutorials on how to get ass. Phoebe's witticisms, and Sam, the other bartender, who called me her fairy godmother, kept an eye out for me, and helped me get into a cab when I got too drunk or the occasional creep circled too close. Steven's delicate poems about the female form, his musings on the breasts of harpies in old 1970s D&D rulebooks. Tiffany, the hardboiled investigative journalist, and her ability to sneak an entire roast chicken with tomato soup into her backpack when we went to the movies. Vera and I losing our minds over trying to meet our separate magazine deadlines together in the middle of the night, her boyfriend accusing us of an illicit affair when, actually, we were just compulsively drinking herbal tea and talking about cats instead of working. Trudy's gaudy quilts and our shared cheesecakes.

It's the million possibilities I saw in each box of light dotting the skyscrapers that night from the balcony at the Chief's penthouse. Smoking pina colada hookah to Katy Perry blasting in my headphones at a dimly lit café while very seriously writing about how to color-coordinate strap-ons and harnesses to your nail polish. That late-night drive across the bridge, sometimes watching the sun rise from the waters. The city, yes. My gray lady.

Maybe I was lonely, but I was not alone. And I was free in the greatest city in the world.

This is love. And I <3 NY.

Chapter
19

The Last Unicorn

After spending half a year learning to be okay with being alone, I restarted my OkCupid profile and began talking to a new girl, Elise. She was pretty, but in a way that did not emit a sense of heady danger or smoldering depression. Pretty in a healthy way. I'd noticed, as I spent ample amounts of time in a hermitage trying to decipher where I was going wrong, that I was attracted to intense, glamorous, and dangerous women. Girls with profile pics that showed off extremely low-cut tops and featured tempting grins with barstools in the background. People who said they had no interest in a relationship. I'd long since given up on finding another lesbian who liked The Elder Scrolls or anything that didn't involve Vegan potlucks or depressing indie rock.

But now I thought, *No. I won't do this any longer. I will only engage with someone who's a real fit, someone who makes me happy. If I have to be alone forever, I'm okay with that. It will all be okay.*

Elise's profile made me smile—she had a handful of pictures dancing, one wearing a Christmas sweater, and she'd written, "I'm looking for a good person. Someone adorable, like me!" We both liked heavy metal and video games, we rated at 98 percent compatibility as friends and lovers, close to 0 percent as enemies. I thought she sounded too perfect; there was no way she could be real. And I found, once again, that she was an editor. I wondered what about the way I'd answered those one hundred profile personality questions matched me with literally every lesbian editor in New York City. Or was it just that every lesbian in New York City was an editor?

Her initial pickup line was cute, simple. "I see you like Evanescence and Rob Zombie. Hot. Who is your favorite *Street Fighter II* character?"

"Ken, baby."

"Ugh, no, it's all about Ryu."

I wondered what this difference said about our personalities. Ken and Ryu were two practically identical characters. But one was flashy and daring, the other cool and mysterious. Would that be us?

We made a date.

I waited for her in a bar that served cupcakes and wine, thinking that just sounded like something out of a rom com. She passed by the bar's front window: a drop-dead, mysterious, dark-eyed beauty. Italian and Puerto Rican, like God himself had taken my two favorite types of girl and put them together in a swirl cone. My breath caught in my throat—but she kept walking. I thought, *Oh, that's not my date, I guess.* Still, I couldn't get the girl who'd walked past the window out of my head. Even though I'd only seen her for a second, I felt a strange undertow of deep sadness, like something important was supposed to have happened, and I'd lost it.

Ten minutes later, she came back and admitted she'd accidentally walked to the wrong bar.

We ate raspberry cupcakes and drank wine. Somehow, over bites, we figured out we both had the same ex. She described a girl she'd seen a few months ago and the fuzzy details became alarmingly clear.

"This girl. She was new to dating women, right? I remember. A virgin. Dead ringer for Mayim Bialik."

"Oh no," Elise said. "She complained to me about her ex, a girl named Esther. I was hoping it wasn't you!"

"Fuck," I said, wondering how long the rest of the date would last.

"Don't get mad, but she said, 'I dated that blogger, Esther, from Broads in the Big Apple. I thought she was weird, and she was the worst sex I've ever had. And I've only slept with one person!'"

"Ha. Awesome. Well, that's great; I'm sure this date is over, and you'd like to get the hell away from me," I said, laughing nervously to the point of insanity.

"No. I like you, and I'm having fun with you. I want to find out for myself," she said, smiling.

I was afraid of what Elise would say next, but apparently when it came to this ex, history had repeated itself.

In the same way the virgin dumped me about a week before Valentine's Day because she wasn't sure if she was a lesbian or not, she'd dated Elise for four months and then, out of the blue, dumped her the night before they were supposed to go to a wine festival that cost Elise $200.

As Elise told me the story, her eyes began to well.

"Like she couldn't have waited until the day after the festival. The bitch!"

"Oh, screw her," I said. "She says I'm weird, but she left a giant blue ass print from her jeans on my living room wall. I can't even watch TV because of it."

"Yeah well, she broke up with me and then left a trail of menstrual blood on my duvet cover. She was on her period, and she was wearing a dress," Elise said.

I hailed our waiter.

"Excuse me, can I have two glasses of champagne?" I said.

The waiter came back, and I raised my glass.

"To not dating Blossom anymore," I said.

"Blossom's loss is our gain!" Elise said.

We talked on and on that night, walking through the city, excitedly exchanging ideas and blurting out questions.

"What are your thoughts on teleportation?" Elise asked.

"My thoughts are that . . . it's cool?" I said.

"But do you think souls can be teleported too? Or just bodies? Like on *Star Trek*."

I laughed.

"I don't know; it's kind of a package deal. I think Jean-Luc Picard had a soul after all of that teleporting, right?"

"Good answer," she said, smiling. "What about the Oxford comma? Pro or con?"

"Pro," I said.

"Thank God. We can keep seeing each other now," she said.

I wanted to take her somewhere fun but not too romantic. I remembered the adage of the girls at the magazine: get some pussy before you invest.

We stopped into The Duplex. Nothing says romance like drag queens who can sing. Plus, Phoebe was working at this bar too, and she always looked out for me on those long nights out. *Jeopardy!* was playing on the TV. Phoebe grinned at us and made Scooby Snacks. She was relieved that I was no longer living in a dark isolated hole in my apartment and was out on an actual date again.

"No need to pay—just enjoy yourself tonight," she said. She leaned in and whispered, "I'm glad to see you're finally moving on. I have a good feeling about this one."

I brought the drinks back to Elise.

"Let's play a game," I said. "If you get the next question right, I'll kiss you. If I get it right, you'll kiss me."

In the end, I don't think either of us got the *Jeopardy!* question right. But I held her close and smooched her. It felt a little like magic. There was something pure in her kiss, something that made it stand out more than the hundreds I'd tasted before. There was something quiet in it. Something that said, "Will you notice me, please?"

She wanted to come home with me. To this day, she won't admit that she was begging for it. I wanted badly to fuck her, but I thought maybe it was time to try something different. Maybe I should attempt this "getting to know someone on a deeper level" business instead of just impulsively flying into their bed like a needy succubus with anxious attachment disorder. I'd already realized during my hermitage that I would be okay whether I was with someone or alone. So taking things slowly wouldn't hurt my chances at all anymore.

I said coyly, "Oh, but I'm not that kind of girl!" Of course, it was a bold-faced lie. But leaping into people's beds didn't seem to be quite a good strategy after all.

A week later we went on a second date. She took me out to a fancy restaurant and then to Barcade, a bar/arcade in Brooklyn. We drank chocolate- and cookie-flavored beers all night while playing games from the '80s. There, we found an odd game called Timber in which two lumberjacks try to chop the highest amount of wood before the quitting clock goes off at the end of their shift. I said, "What game here would be more appropriate for a couple of lesbians?" We laughed about the terrible graphics until we were out of breath. Soon we were both tipsy, cheeks ruddy, and she kissed me—then asked again if I wanted to come home with her. This time, I couldn't play the coy Christian virgin because it had already taken an astronomical amount of restraint not to go home with her on date number one.

With Juliet, sex was very chemical and primal. With Elise, it was more emotional and mental. Maybe it was the way she held me. She wasn't dirty, just honest.

I threw her down and took my time kissing and nibbling, paying attention to every inch of her body. Every time I made her come, her breath would catch in these little adoring sighs, and I could feel all over that she really wanted me. She let me see into her soul, her touch sparked all over as aether, the fifth element—the force of the gods. She was someone who gave energy, whereas I just burned it. The very essence of joy, the sliver of the heavens tucked hidden inside the clouds. Something blossomed in my heart. I realized that it was hope.

We lay down cuddling, and I started to doze a little. Suddenly she tapped my shoulder.

"Psst," she whispered in the dark. "Are you awake?"

I didn't say anything; I wanted to see what she would say.

"I never did something like this before. I mean go home with someone on the second date."

I stayed quiet.

"I like you."

"I like you too," I said, pulling her close.

In the morning, she said, "I have a surprise for you. Just sit there, on the couch."

She emerged from the kitchen with two plates of eggs, bacon, and toast, and I realized in a very hilariously sad way that no girl had ever made me breakfast before. No girl had ever even given me cab fare before. We ate together quietly and looked out at the city from her balcony. I rested my head on her shoulder, and I felt like I belonged there. Like this was going to be something that would last. It seemed odd, to feel something intuitively like that. I felt it instinctively, in the same way I knew whenever I'd just had my last hookup with someone.

We kept seeing each other, slowly getting close. I was defensive for the first few months. If I didn't hear from her for a good portion of the day, or if I heard her talking about a close female friend, I'd start to get suspicious. I thought, *So when will it happen? When are the drugs, the drinking, the verbal abuse, the random men or ex-girlfriends going to become a problem?*

After a month had passed, I stayed the night and woke up with pink eye. I'd tried so hard to be suave and seductive, getting dressed in my fancy black cocktail dresses, trying to say all the right words. Playing the virgin instead of the vamp. And now here I was, in Elise's bathroom, with slime gushing out of my swollen eye. Biding for time so she'd never see it.

I heard a knock on the door.

"Are you okay in there? You've been in there for a while."

Oh great, I thought. *Now she either thinks I'm dead or taking a shit. This isn't going to end well for anybody.*

I decided to just get it over with, like ripping off a Band-Aid. I burst out of the bathroom door like the Kool-Aid man and covered half of my face, shouting, "Look away! Look away!" before explaining that I had pink eye and she shouldn't touch any doorknobs or pillow cases without gloves.

"Hmm. Pink eye," she said. "Isn't that, like, where a person gets fecal matter on their eyelids?"

I cringed. "I swear to you that I wash my hands. Each and every time."

Elise shrugged. "Well, I've never had it! Okay, I'll try to be careful."

She helped me to the closest subway while I turned my head away from her. She said I was like the phantom from *The Phantom of the Opera.* Somehow, I was able to hobble to the nearest doctor, but not before a gentleman of the streets came up behind me and said, "Damn, girl. That ass though. Can I get your number?"

I turned and stared at him with my bulging, pus-laden eye.

"God d*amn*! That shit is fucked up!" he cried, running away from me.

I thought that would be the last I'd ever hear from Elise. But she called that night and said she'd been worried all day about whether or not I got home safely. And she wanted to see me again.

On date five or six, at a fancy Italian restaurant, we were chatting while waiting for the waiter to arrive. Elise leaned in close and took my hand.

"So, how many people did you sleep with before me?"

"Do we really have to talk about it?"

"I'd really like to know."

I started to fidget with my necklace, looking around the room for any kind of distraction. You can never really tell what the reaction will be when confessing this kind of thing to a woman. Either she'll adore your prowess or be scared shitless.

"I know this is going to sound bad, but I kind of lost track a while ago," I said, taking an extra-large sip of my drink. Elise's eyes grew wide.

"You lost *track* of how many people you've slept with?"

"No! I, ah, I just mean that it's more than twenty, and either at or less than thirty. I think."

"You've slept with *thirty* people?!"

I started to haggle the number downward, as if we were contestants on *The Price Is Right*.

"I didn't say it was thirty! I said it was probably less than thirty. It could have been twenty-four, maybe."

"*Twenty-four people*?!"

"Okay! I got it. It was twenty-two."

"Twenty-two?! I'm gonna be sick."

"You're going to be *sick*? This was over the course of twelve years of my life! I didn't bang twenty—or, maybe thirty—people a night! God! Is that not a reasonable number for twelve years?"

"It's just a lot of people. It just sounds like a lot of people. I don't know, I don't want to think about it."

"Well how many people did you sleep with?" I asserted angrily.

"*Four*. I'm a nice Catholic Italian gal from Long Island. What kind of girl do you think I am?"

Staring uncomfortably out the window, I briefly thought of launching myself through the glass as though we were in an action movie, stop drop 'n rolling on the sidewalk to shake the shards off my dress, and running as fast as possible down the sidewalk for a solid thirty minutes. How much distance would that cover?

I tried to salvage the situation.

"I'm not a giant whore or anything! Only when the mood calls for it. Which . . . being with you totally calls for it. Did I tell you that you look so cute tonight?"

Elise frowned uncomfortably.

The waiter, and my cavalry, arrived.

"So um . . . who wants bruschetta?"

After she'd seen slime gush out of my eye and I'd given her a slut-induced panic attack, I truly thought this woman would never call me again.

She just kept on calling.

A part of me said I should be afraid. That nothing in this life comes for free or without a price. Maybe I should flee in terror now, avoid the heartache later. It would only be a matter of time until she wanted another woman (or man) and would ask if I were cool with just being a side piece. Nothing this good could last for no reason. Maybe she only wanted me for the sex because I'd been her first rapid-fire hookup, and now the oxytocin had her confused. Perhaps it would wear off, and in its wake would be nothing but regret.

It felt like every time I tried to be open, tried to love, one of the same few scenarios happened: the girl would want another lover and ask if I was cool letting her fuck somebody else and hearing all about it, or her ex from 903 years ago would all of a sudden give her a call, and she'd go back out with them, having a change of heart. Or she'd just realize that the way she felt about me was fleeting, and I'd be left holding the bag. *No*, I told myself. *I'd better get out of here before I get all fucked up again. It will happen. And I'll be crying on the fire escape again while my upstairs neighbors have loud sex for an entire five to ten minutes, secretly hoping that my obscene, disgusting wailing will kill their mood.*

Another part of me realized that it was not in my nature to be afraid of anything, least of all love. This fear—these thoughts—had been taught to me. To know fear was not my birthright.

But all those things I worried about never happened with Elise. The years went on. We endured many hardships and illnesses in our families together. And we endured them with the same curious and playful spirit we'd once had while wandering the city and talking about whether or not extraterrestrials could be real. Terrible things happened. Months after we started dating, her brother became ill with terminal cancer. Then my mother ended up in a mental hospital and became homeless. Then I had a cancer scare. Turned out to be Lyme. But Elise didn't turn and flee. She continued to love me for literally no reason, even when I bought a slide whistle and a whoopie cushion just to save our own sanity through all of the suffering.

After three years in her arms, I knew she was the one; we'd passed every test together, and when things got rough, we ran toward each other instead of away. I knew that I never again wanted to roam the dark streets of the city alone. Here was someone who loved me even when I had unwaxed eyebrows, even when I was wearing Ninja Turtle pajama pants. Who loved me for more than just sex but saw the sex as an added bonus, like having a fun job with health insurance and a 401(k).

Eventually, I planned our next adventure: a trip to Prague, where I proposed to Elise on the rooftop of an old European castle under the moonlight. During every dinner course we ate that night before I popped the question, I felt like I was going to faint and die; I was so scared she'd say no.

Elise was the fairest of all, the one with the gentlest eyes and the bravest heart. I knew there was no one in this world who could love me with more ferocity. I thought, *Out of every human being on this planet, how lucky I am to have found you, to love and be loved by you. To even be in your presence. For you, I would do and be anything. I pledge my life into your hands. For you, I am willing to risk the humiliation of being rejected and place a ring of faith on your finger, if you'll have it. How many women are there in this world who love with something as gaudy as just passion or even out of fear of being alone. Only you are capable of loving with fortitude. I'm nothing but a lowly serf to you, so I pledge my fealty. May I serve you and do nothing but please you for the rest of our lives.*

I got on one knee and put a black diamond ring on her finger. She said yes and burst into tears. Then I started laughing and crying at the same time, so happy that our love had been given a chance to live.

Chapter
20

My Heart Will Go On

I hadn't heard from Morgan in nearly eight years. And all I got was an email that said, "I think I want something from Harry Potter."

Puzzled, I reread the email. Was there some kind of deeper meaning? What did she mean by "Harry?" By "Potter?" By "something?" I thought about it, then concluded that she must have emailed the wrong Esther. But could there be that many people with my name? *Hmm.*

Not knowing what else to do, I emailed back the most apt Potter quote I could find: "The scar had not pained Harry for nineteen years. All was well." [1]

Within minutes, my phone buzzed again. She said she was sorry, that she'd intended to email her tattoo artist (also named Esther). Then she nervously LOLed and asked what I was up to.

It all seemed bizarre to me. No acknowledgement of the secret marriage or completely ghosting me. As if psychically wound-

---

[1] J. K. Rowling, Harry Potter and the Deathly Hallows (London: Bloomsbury, 2014), 620.

ing and jilting me to the point where I'd move across the country hadn't ever happened. At first, I thought about deleting the email or just ignoring it. But I couldn't resist snapping up the bait.

"Nothing much," I said. "I'm living in New York now. And just planning my wedding. I'm getting married in a few months. It sure is a lot more work than I'd anticipated. But I was so happy to go dress shopping. It feels like all of my dreams are coming true."

Send!

To throw the wedding in her face was incredibly juvenile. But when I thought about the nights I'd wandered the city during blizzard weather, or the night that I threw away the Smittens, it didn't feel undeserved. On so many nights, I would cry as I worked on my romance novel and musical, *The Bridesmaid*, about a single, depressed woman who makes it her entire MO to destroy as many weddings as possible in a blind rage. Unbeknownst to me, my novel became reality as my own planner faded into the background, and I found myself doing more and more of the legwork to pull off my own wedding. It seems Karma always has her way with you.

Ding!

"Wow, married! Congratulations!" she said. She wrote another paragraph admitting she was wrong and sorry for everything she'd done. Then, "Well, believe it or not, I'm going to be in New York tomorrow." She continued, "Before you get married . . . let me take you to dinner. I know a very nice restaurant in the city."

I nearly fell off my chair. What was this madness? I couldn't tell whether or not she was trying to sweep me off my feet in a last-minute attempt to sabotage the wedding.

I was sitting at my computer with my mouth wide open like a carp when Elise asked me what was going on.

"Well, Morgan busted on in," I said. "She apparently wants to either take me to a fine dining establishment to make amends or . . . who knows."

Elise shrugged. "What do you want for dinner?"

I flew backward, punctuating the air with hand gestures.

"The woman who demolished me mentally in the prime of my youth just asked me out to dinner, out of nowhere, after eight years. You're not shocked?"

Elise shrugged again.

"I have a feeling that you won't leave me for her, so I'm not worried about it," she said, rolling her eyes.

It wasn't the reaction I was hoping for. I craved a telenovela-style blowout where she'd have angry sex with me on the floor of the apartment to prove her dominance. Still, her quiet and secure resolve showed me how different she was from my other partners.

"Well, I'm cooking pasta," Elise said. I went back to my computer.

I thought again about those nights when I was sure I wouldn't make it, or that I'd never love again, obsessed with the idea that Morgan and I were star-crossed. And I finally realized she never loved me. At least, not in a healthy way. Nearly a decade later, I empathized with her in a way that I couldn't have in the hateful passion of my youth. Something happened between us, something that sparked a visceral attraction, and regardless of whatever lies or truths she told me, I think she just got caught up at some point. It never even occurred to me that she could have lied out of the fear of losing me. I still don't know whether the girl I loved was a real person or just a hologram. But I do know that something powerful happened between us, something that inoculated me against the disbelief of romantic love and changed my life forever.

My fingers twitched above the keyboard for a while as I wondered what to say. I realized finally that there were no words. Too many things had happened over the past decade. In the same way I couldn't be sure I'd ever loved the real her, the woman she loved didn't exist anymore. My drive and my lustfulness had tempered, but so, too, had my selfishness and propensity for drama. Elise's stability and calm, healthy love came without compromises, ebbs, or flows. She gentled me. There was still a tiny part of me that said, "Cut Morgan down. Cut her wide open where she stands— for everything that she did to you. You have the high ground." But the other part remembered those snowy nights alone in the city. How being alone in the world felt like dying. And a bigger part said *I'm not that girl anymore.*

Eventually, I took a breath, then typed, "I think enough time has passed that I can wish you happiness. Whether it's with a man or a woman." Then I closed my laptop.

It was too late now to explain everything that had happened in eight years. But not too late to start again.

Chapter
21

Say Yes
to the
Dress

Never in my life did I think that planning a wedding could be so much work. In my head, I envisioned booking a venue and enough food for one hundred plus people. But I suddenly understood why some women begin to plan out the color of their napkins and matching invitations at birth. My only rules for success seemed to be: (1) everyone shows up, (2) nobody gets drunk to the point of throwing up on the floor, and (3) nothing gets set on fire. That should be an excellent wedding.

A wedding is a rite of passage for many women, one in which they either grow much closer (or further apart) from their own mothers. Despite being rather femme, I'd accepted long ago that I was terrible at actually being a female. I still don't know how to dress myself. Generally, I choose black pants and a black shirt (thinking that's impossible to mess up), along with a burgundy accent of some sort (because that makes me feel sexy). As long as my clothes cover my ass and don't have any holes in them, I pray for social acceptance and walk out the door.

What did I know of floral arrangements? Lighting? Hairdos? Table arrangements? The whole thing was a mystery to me. I myself had been to very few weddings, and my favorite one involved my best friend since second grade marching down the aisle in lockstep with six Stormtroopers to "The Imperial March." That, to me, was the epitome of good taste.

I wished that I could reach out to my mother, feeling a deep-seated insecurity of the feminine arts. Elise at several junctures thought we could just elope and leave the whole thing behind. My mom was in and out of the mental hospital that year, hearing voices and insisting that a being called "Monstrance" was trying to tell her about the true path to God. I knew that she wasn't in any condition to talk about hors d'oeuvres. When I wasn't planning the wedding, I felt that I was the one going insane from calling different homeless shelters for her and trying to find one that had any special help or assistance for a woman of her age. I was trying to prepare because I could tell that she'd overstayed her three-year welcome at my aunt's house and that, any day, she'd be on the streets.

Inside, I longed for the naggy mother. The one with the shrill voice who demands something dated like shrimp scampi be served. I wanted her to help save the day and to give me a big, sappy speech about seeing her little girl grow up. I wanted the TV mom. Instead, I hired a wedding planner with a drinking problem who ranted about not being able to find the right man in New York City. She kept racy boudoir photos of herself in leather hanging on the wall of her bedroom as we talked about printers for the envelopes. *Wow*, I thought. *Can't imagine why you're still single.*

I realized that I had to seize control of the wedding about five months before the date, when the planner sent us to a "venue" that turned out to be the place where The Hilton stored all their trash during the day. It smelled like hot garbage and had stains all over the floor, and our hostess had the nerve to tell us that they'd light candles and get rid of the smell "for your special day." Then she asked, "Do you have any questions?"

"Yeah," I said, before I could even control the words coming out of my mouth. "Where the fuck is the exit?"

The day came when I had to shop for a dress. I dreaded it and told my cousin I could only get excited about the prospect if I thought about it like playing an RPG.

"Think of it as bridal armor," she said. "Will you choose light or heavy? Are you a battlemage? An archer?"

Honestly, I didn't even know where to go to buy a dress. It was then that someone stepped in to save the day, and it wasn't my mother.

My mother-in-law offered to come with me to a fancy bridal boutique on Fifth Avenue. Suddenly, things were looking up! An over-achieving Capricorn with every to-do list on an impeccably placed Post-it note in my corner. Barbara was the opposite of my mother in every way. My mother cowered under the weight of depression and codependency. Barbara was strongly self-reliant and never let anyone tell her what to do. My mom would waver in her indecisiveness until the decision was made for her or the opportunity to do anything had passed. Barbara was assertive and would keep pushing ahead through anything, immediately after making a choice that would take her all but five seconds to mull through. Yet Barbara was warm and genuine. My mother would give a thousand hugs and kisses, then mysteriously vanish when she was actually required to show up. Barbara came across as strong and confident but not aloof—I knew with her in my corner, the wedding was back on track.

We met at the boutique, and I looked around at all of the other girls, in tow with their many chick friends and bossy mothers.

They had nasal accents and all seemed to come from New Jersey. I wondered why no brides were coming in hot from Manhattan. For but a breath, I felt sadness that my mom wasn't there, but when I turned and looked into Barbara's eyes and smiled, I knew everything would be okay.

Our assistant introduced herself and was missing a tooth. I tried not to look at it when she smiled. While we waited, I got to know the receptionist, a goth woman who secretly liked Nine Inch Nails but was forced to play the soundtrack to *Beauty and the Beast* and other such nonsense to help straight women feel like their storybook dreams were coming true. I asked her to please blast Rob Zombie if I found anything that didn't look terrible on me.

Somehow, I had no important instructions or descriptions for what I wanted the dress to look like. I whispered to the assistant, "I want a white dress, even if we all know I don't deserve it anymore," and she hissed a laugh through her toothy gap.

She kept bringing me mermaid dresses. I didn't know anything about the art of womanhood, but I knew that I would rather pass away quietly in noble indignity before ever wearing a mermaid dress in front of another human being. We all walked through racks of dresses as I pointed here and there to ones I liked. She'd bring another mermaid dress that was supposed to accentuate my tits but instead acted as a bra for my third stomach.

"Just stop!" Barbara cried in a shrill Long Island accent, the magnitude and authority of which could only rival Patrick Henry declaring, "Give me liberty, or give me death!"

"My daughter-in-law doesn't want a friggin' mermaid dress! We said that already! So help me God if you send us one more mermaid dress. Try listening to what the girl actually wants!"

The assistant slithered away, surprisingly to get the dress that I wanted. And it turned out to be the only one I liked.

"Barbara, let's go get dessert somewhere close," I said. If I knew anything about Barbara, it was her great love of Entenmann's paired with sweet coffee.

We found a small place nearby and ordered tiramisu with two spoons to split. She asked where my mom was, why she wasn't involved with the wedding. I was ashamed to tell her about my mother's mental illness. My family was a constant source of shame for me. It was precisely because both of my parents were always going to the nuthouse, digging their way out of Chapter 7 bankruptcy, or making general spectacles of themselves that I tried so hard to be an all-American girl next door. I wanted to work hard and create a normal, stable life free of their histrionics, to prove that I could be different than them. Once, in therapy, my shrink had me make a list of the necessary qualities I needed in the right life partner. I wrote, "Must come from an equally bad family."

She laughed and said, "Esther, why would you say that? You do know that people from bad families tend to be . . . abusers, right?"

"Well, it doesn't seem fair," I said. "When you marry someone, you accept not only them but also their family. How fair would it be to somebody if they had a normal, functional family and I gave them mine in return?"

She paused, smiled sadly, and leaned back in her chair. "So, fair in your thinking. But don't you think you deserve better than what you came from? Are you being fair to yourself?"

It took me a long time to let that lesson sink in.

I blurted everything out to Barbara. About my mother and the psychotic depression. My dad and the abuse. Her selfishness and inability to feel empathy for me.

"I'm sorry; it's embarrassing," I said.

Barbara paused. "You're not alone. And there's no reason for you to feel embarrassed about what your parents did," she said.

187

She told me about her own background and how her relationship with her mom was very similar to my own.

"So it seems both our mothers were friggin' idiots," she concluded. "It's a miracle that you and I not only survived—we thrived in spite of it."

I finished the last bite of tiramisu and smiled at her. I didn't have to hide anything anymore. We joked about how quickly we'd gotten everything done. Barbara was biracial like me (half German, half Puerto Rican.) We made fun of our obsessively efficient German sides. Having dessert with Barbara . . . it was the first time I felt what it was like to have a good mother. Someone I could look up to, confide in and identify with. How sad that I was nearly thirty-four before feeling that way. The old punchline goes something like, "Take my mother-in-law—*please!*" Not so with me. I'd argue, "Take my mother-in-law—*over my dead body.*"

Under Barbara's guidance, the rest of the wedding planning went smoothly. I planned a '90s wedding, and, with all of its neon and whimsy, at times it felt like a child's birthday party and not a celebration for two grown women in love.

When it was my turn to walk down the aisle, I went with my uncle. After all, my father was dead, and I had no idea if my mother would be strapped to a bed and sedated somewhere. She recovered in time for the wedding but spent most of the days leading up to it talking about herself.

During my big day, she asked no less than four times, "What's your wife's name again? I just can't seem to remember." I had to restrain myself from screaming in public. But every now and then, I'd look over, see Barbara across the room, and smile. My new father-in-law, so quiet and gentle, came up to tap me on the shoulder.

"We love you and would never do anything to hurt you, honey. I just wanted you to know that," he said with a smile. It was a new concept for me: to be part of a family, to be cared for by one.

Elise taught me at the eleventh hour that it's never too late to fall in love again. And Barbara taught me that it's never too late to find your family in this world, if you weren't born with a good one. Elise's father was kind when mine was cruel. And in the loneliness of my childhood, I'd had no other children to talk to. Now I had her sister, a witty and gregarious woman with a sassy sense of humor. From the moment I met Laura, I knew I had to get to know her better. Without hesitation, the first time I met her she threw her arms around me.

"So, you're a writer!" Laura exclaimed in a pronounced Long Island accent. "Ever heard of Ruby Dixon?"

"No," I said.

"She writes paranormal romance. I read this great series about a planet full of blue-skinned, sexy barbarian aliens that seduce a space colony of women. Phenomenal."

"Aliens? Like little green men?" I shouted, throwing my hands in the air. She giggled.

"Nothin' little or green about *these* men, let me tell yous."

"I love it. Let's start a book club," I said.

When we went to the courthouse, I took Elise's name and left my old life behind.

Chapter
22

The Last Call

Time encroached. I was bound in holy matrimony, and my wife dragged me kicking and screaming to New Jersey so we could buy a house and live the American dream.

"You can drag a girl to Jersey," I grumbled at the time. "But you can't make her go full burb."

My existence as a hausfrau was quiet, paling in contrast to the nights where I'd taken photos of celesbians at red-carpet events, tried to be glamorous at bars, wandered the streets until three o'clock in the morning, or stayed up late proofreading feature articles with the Chief. Now my concerns for the day involved taking stock of the remaining toilet paper and contacting the landscapers about mowing the backyard. Hearing the sounds of other people's giggling children running around while hunting for freelance work in my office, instead of loud neighbors having sex or drunk people throwing up outside my bedroom window.

I sat down with a cup of tea to begin my work. Suddenly, my phone lit up. It was the Chief, incoming.

"Hello?"

"Juliet's dead." She sighed.

Silence punctuated the air between us.

"No," I said.

"She's dead," the Chief repeated.

My breath caught in my throat. Part of me was shocked, yet the other part was not surprised at all. I think I'd known ever since that night when we fought over her suicide attempt that one day it would end this way. But I'd hoped it wouldn't happen. That everything would be all right. She'd find true love, get sober, move to another part of Jersey, and perhaps become a PTA lesbian soccer mom with one of her many suitors that stirred her heart. She'd have two little blonde kids she would overshare photos of on Facebook.

"I don't know what to say," I said.

"There's nothing to say. I just wanted you to know before you found out on Facebook."

"Tell me that she didn't feel much pain when it happened? That it didn't hurt too badly?" To even say those words left me winded. "Please tell me she didn't kill herself."

"She didn't kill herself," the Chief said.

"How did it happen?"

"She went to sleep, and she never woke up," the Chief said. "Let's leave it at that."

I knew better than to press much more, and it didn't take a great stretch of the imagination to figure out what she meant. I thought about the time I'd googled Juliet a year ago and had found her public blog post about how she'd tried to kill herself two more times—once again with the pills and once by slashing her wrists with a pocketknife.

"I want you to know that we're having a memorial in her honor within the next few days. And I want you to be prepared—her lover will be there, and she knows all about what happened between you two. Juliet saved your old text messages and letters, and she discovered them. Rather recently. So she's not a big fan of you being there. But I think you have a right to be."

Over and over, Juliet had told me I was just a fuck buddy, just a toy. Never once did I think she would have kept our correspondences for seven years. For a short while, I kept mine too. Eventually, I deleted them all because I wanted to forget about her and pretend it never happened. Then I felt a sudden rush of bloodlust. This woman had kept Juliet on the side as a mistress for five whole years. How many times did Juliet sob into my bare breasts late at night that all she'd ever wanted was her, her, her . . . and not me?

"I'm so sorry that she can't handle some sexts from seven years ago," I said. "That must be really hard for her."

"Esther! Juliet's dead, okay! Let it go. There are maybe three other people Juliet hooked up with coming to the memorial, and her lover is not happy about any of it."

"God, Chief," I said. "This is the ninth circle of lesbian hell. I can't go to a memorial where everybody fucked the deceased. This will be like that episode of *The Golden Girls* where they went to a funeral and found out that they'd all slept with the same guy."

I heard a smile on the other end of the phone.

"It all ended in twenty-two minutes, and the episode had a happy sitcom ending, did it not? A good time was had by all, fun for the whole family. Come to the memorial. I gotta go. Bye."

I checked my calendar and realized the memorial was the day after my thirty-seventh birthday. I thought about all of those late-night conversations Juliet and I had where we bared our souls about the intense abuse we both lived through as children, and I wondered: *Why does one of us have the right to live, and the other does not?* We were so similar and yet so opposite. She always wanted to drown in the sadness of her past; I avoided thinking about the past at all costs and used it to push forward. We both balanced on a razor's edge; we both used humor and art to escape. If I'd had less emotional endurance, it could have easily been me in the ground.

What makes one person weak and the other strong? I still don't think I know the answer to that question, and I never will.

The day came, and I walked to the address I'd been given. The memorial was held in one of Juliet's favorite bars.

I saw John, the old art director at the magazine. He was a sassy gay man, the only guy on a staff of savvy and witty lesbians. We hugged each other so tightly that my eyes felt like they were going to pop out as we excitedly shared about our current lovers. It felt like no time at all had passed since I'd last seen him. Chris, the distribution manager and party promoter, sauntered up. Once one of the toughest and most powerful butches I knew, she still had the same presence and now walked slowly with a cane. We hugged like life depended on it and slowly walked up the stairs to the event together. I wanted her to go first because of her cane. Ever gallant, she would not dare go ahead of a femme.

I watched Chris and the Chief hug, and I realized a golden era of lesbian nightlife might die with us. I was one of the younger people there, and I was almost forty. I wondered how young lesbians would find love in this new world of dating apps. It wouldn't be like in my day, getting wasted at bars and dealing with catty gossip, trying to keep your head up. Now you swiped left or right on a phone screen to determine a person's worthiness of love via physical attractiveness.

I thought about the very first night I met Juliet at Stonewall, how I was drawn to her magnetically and how it was confusing to be enchanted by a blonde. Her humor, her breezy yet mysterious nature and flirty laugh, hooked me. And she'd admitted that she didn't like other femmes at all; she had a thing for athletic tomboys. If we'd seen each other on an app, would we have even met up in person? Maybe not.

Then Juliet's longtime lover walked into the room. The Chief tried to introduce us, but the other woman refused and turned her back to me. I'd heard so much about her for the entire year I dated Juliet that I'd imagined Botticelli's *The Birth of Venus*. Now I just saw a broken woman about ten years my senior, disheveled in grief. All those nights I'd burned with hatred for someone I'd never even met, wanting revenge—it all seemed so long ago, so petty. I looked at her across the room as she glared, and I didn't feel anything but sorry for her.

I sat with John and Chris as we shared our favorite stories about Juliet.

"She liked you a lot," John said.

It was news to me. I felt like we'd had so many fights that maybe Juliet hated my guts.

"She told me all the time how smart you were and how she felt impressed by you. And . . . she gave me all the details. You know what I mean."

My face ran hot.

"What can I say?" John continued. "She loved you in a lot of ways!"

I blushed again and averted his gaze.

Whether or not she just saw me as a fuck buddy, Juliet made me feel beautiful again. Never had I been wanted with such intense desire and actually reciprocated it. To be chased with such primal and animalistic passion felt like a force of nature, even if it wasn't marriage material.

"I always felt stupid around her," I said. "She complained that my bookshelf was too small. Boasted that she loved to read Dostoevsky and that my taste was 'pedestrian.' I don't think she listened any of the one million times that I told her I had to sell all my books to make my bags light enough to move to New York."

Chris interjected, "Oh, I schooled her on Dostoevsky. She thought she could highbrow me, not knowing my major was Russian literature. She did complain about your bookshelf though." Chris continued, "But you mostly had lesbian stuff, right? She told me what was on there. I told her she didn't even know what *Rubyfruit Jungle* was, so she had no right to judge you."

The bartender asked us what we were having. I thought about that very first night I met Juliet, how she'd teased me for ordering a cosmo.

"I'll have a cosmopolitan, please!" A few other people thought it was funny and ordered them too. I thought Juliet was rolling around in her grave every time we clinked another glass.

Another girl walked into the bar. It was Diana, her best friend growing up in Jersey. She'd ridden the train all the way from Washington, DC, to celebrate her friend's life. I'd heard Juliet speak so enthusiastically about this girl that I knew everything about her before even having met her. In the photos from their youth, she seemed flashy, dangerous, and exciting. Now she was just a portly, unassuming woman waiting for a drink in poorly chosen footwear.

I ran up to her and said hello. She excitedly told stories about the two of them growing up, and she felt somehow familiar. I never let on that Juliet told me they were best friends and occasional fuck buddies, who vowed one day to get married at fifty if they hadn't found anybody else. Diana and I talked about our wives, and we arrogantly swapped photos of the women we loved with pride.

"Your wife is hot."

"Your wife is also hot."

Suddenly, the Coach tapped on her glass.

"Attention, everybody. A toast! Love is like taking a shit or farting. If you loved Juliet, let it all out!"

No one laughed. Members of Juliet's family looked horrified. An uncomfortable stillness filled the room.

Diana and I talked more about her and Juliet's childhood, and it briefly felt like someone had summoned Juliet back from the dead. Sometimes you meet two friends who are nearly twins in personality and inseparable. Wherever one goes, the other one follows. I determined that was Diana and Juliet. To find the friend version of soulmates in this lifetime is so rare. I felt they were lucky to have known it when they did.

Someone put up a poster board with pictures of the two of them.

"It doesn't feel real," Diana said. "I keep feeling like she'll walk up those stairs, any minute now. Just say, 'Haha guys! I'm not really dead!'"

She looked up at the poster board and let out a small, broken-hearted sigh, then touched her hand to her heart.

"Oh," she breathed.

"I hadn't talked to Juliet in a while. The last time we spoke, I yelled terrible things," I said. "We had a falling out. I feel so guilty. I'll never get to take my words back. I'll never get to apologize to her."

It was a relief to finally say those words aloud instead of holding them in. I thought about the night I'd told her she used "people and pills like crutches" and called her a weak person. No anger could have ever justified that.

Diana put her hand on my shoulder.

"Hey. It's all right. Toward the end, she pushed everyone away. One by one. Don't be so hard on yourself." Then Diana said, "I want to go out for a smoke, but I don't smoke anymore."

"Well, I never smoked habitually, but now I wish I did," I said. We went outside, and the Chief joined us.

"Isn't it funny," the Chief said dryly, "that Juliet fucked so many people at the memorial, and her lover only knows about Esther?" She took one last puff and tossed the cigarette onto the ground.

"Does she even know about me?" Diana asked. The Chief grinned and said not a word. Diana walked over to the dying embers and crushed them under shoes awarded solely for both age and comfort.

"Is no one aware that I fucked her for twenty years?!" she screamed.

A whoop of laughs erupted from the balcony above and drowned out her voice.

No one else heard what Diana said. But I did.

I looked at the clock and realized it was nearly midnight. Awfully late for a Jersey hausfrau to be out on the town. I went back into the bar to say goodbye to everybody and shake hands with a few more people. I met the new *GRL* dating columnist: a girl more talented, wittier, younger, and prettier than I was, and instantly loved her. Long ago, I'd known what my fate would be as a short-lived lesbian sex and dating blogger. We all eventually find love, get old, fat, and lose our looks. Use the listicle we wrote about fourteen ways to "drive your girlfriend wild" to try new things on our wives, who probably sometimes wish we wouldn't. This was the part where I shined a flashlight under my chin and shrieked, "This could happen to you!"

The new dating columnist introduced me to the new intern, a fresh-faced twenty-two-year-old who had just moved to the city from the South.

"I love everything about the magazine!" she enthused, eyes sparkling. "Writing for *GRL*, it all feels so glamorous!"

I gave her a big hug and slap on the shoulder.

"The way you feel about the city now, it can only happen once. Enjoy it. I hope all of your dreams come true. And you find everything you could ever want," I said.

I hobbled my way out of the bar. The Chief was still outside smoking.

"I'm gonna call you an Uber," she said.

"Well, I live in New Jersey now, and I'm about thirty to forty minutes out of the city. I think that would be pretty pricey."

"I'm gonna call you an Uber; you just get in the car,"

"I can't accept this."

"Then pretend it's not from me. This one's on Juliet," the Chief said. "She always knew how to get out of paying her tab, didn't she?"

The Chief's eyes became wet, and she gave me a big hug. When I first met her, she seemed larger than life. Now I realized she was two inches shorter than me, but she still loomed greater, even after all of these years.

"I still can't believe she's gone. I don't have much gas left in the tank, kiddo," she said.

"You can get through anything. You are the Chief," I said.

She threw up her hands with a smile, exhausted from years of hearing her unwanted moniker.

"Don't call me Chief," she said softly.

The car rolled up, and I waved goodbye.

He drove through the city and over the George Washington Bridge. It was just like all of those nights I went over the Queensboro Bridge and stared out at the inky waters underneath, wondering if I would ever meet a sweet girl. Now I had to take this car over another river, to another life. A new beginning. I wanted to go home, to a fixer-upper from 1920 that frequently required me to repair two more things every time one thing broke, and just hold my wife.

You are my home now, I thought. We rolled up to the door, and the porch light was still on. I walked upstairs, kissed her forehead as she slept, rolled onto my back, and stared at the ceiling, thinking about how the old days were now finally put to rest.

I thought about the times I'd haunted the Village or the Castro and went home alone, not once thinking something like this could ever happen. Four nights a week I was out there partying, drinking, hunting, loving, lusting. I was the sadist and the masochist, the dom and the sub, the cheater and the cheated. For a while, I went in too deep. Like so many girls, all trying so hard for so many different reasons. So many New York women with not a lot of heart or time to spare.

For about five minutes, I was the Queen of Gay Street. No, really. I was.

Esther Mollica

has written for *Wired*, *GO*, *Bust*, *Curve*, *Autostraddle* and *The Bay Area Reporter*. Her short romantic comedy, *Never the Bride*, was featured as one of four films by up-and-coming women of color in San Francisco's Frameline Film Festival, 2010.

In 2011 she was named, "New York's Most Eligible Lesbian Bachelorette" by *Time Out New York*, which ironically almost scared off her wife.

9 798986 958118